E-Mail Rules

Other Books by Nancy Flynn

The ePolicy Handbook: Designing and Implementing Effective E-Mail, Internet, and Software Policies (AMACOM)

Writing Effective E-Mail: Improving Your Electronic Communication

E-Mail Rules

A Business Guide
to Managing Policies,
Security, and Legal Issues,
for E-Mail and Digital Communications

**Nancy Flynn
and
Randolph Kahn, Esq.**

AMACOM

American Management Association

New York • Atlanta • Brussels • Buenos Aires • Chicago • London • Mexico City •
San Francisco • Shanghai • Tokyo • Toronto • Washington, D.C.

Special discounts on bulk quantities of AMACOM books are
available to corporations, professional associations, and other
organizations. For details, contact Special Sales Department,
AMACOM, a division of American Management Association,
1601 Broadway, New York, NY 10019.
Tel.: 212-903-8316. Fax: 212-903-8083.
Web site: www.amacombooks.org

This publication is designed to provide accurate and authoritative
information in regard to the subject matter covered. It is sold with
the understanding that neither the publisher nor the authors are
engaged in rendering legal, accounting, or other professional service.
If legal advice or other expert assistance is required, the services of a
competent professional person should be sought.

Library of Congress Cataloging-in-Publication Data

Flynn, Nancy, 1956-
    E-mail rules : a business guide to managing policies, security, and
legal issues for e-mail and digital communication / Nancy Flynn and
Randolph Kahn.
        p.   cm.
    Includes bibliographical references and index.
    ISBN 0-8144-7188-9
    1. Electronic mail system—Management.   2. Electronic mail
system—Security measures.   3. Electronic records—Management.
I. Title: Email rules.   II. Kahn, Randolph.   III. Title.

HE7551 .F578 2003
384.3'4'068—dc21

                                                          2002152888

Printing number

10   9   8   7   6   5   4   3   2   1

Contents

Preface xiii

Acknowledgments xv

PART ONE
The Case for E-Mail Management 1

 Chapter 1: Introduction
 E-Mail Rule #1: Strategic E-Mail Management
  Reduces Liabilities 3

 Chapter 2: Real-World Legal Issues
 E-Mail Rule #2: Manage Employees' E-Mail Use 12

 Chapter 3: E-Mail Ownership and Cybertheft
 E-Mail Rule #3: E-Mail Belongs to the Employer, Not
  the Employee 20

PART TWO
Designing and Implementing Effective
E-Mail Policies 25

 Chapter 4: Why Implement E-Mail Policies?
 E-Mail Rule #4: E-Mail Can Come Back to Haunt You 27

Chapter 5: E-Mail Privacy
E-Mail Rule #5: There Is No One-Size-Fits-All E-Mail
   Policy   30

Chapter 6: E-Mail Content
E-Mail Rule #6: Control Risk by Controlling Content   33

Chapter 7: Netiquette
E-Mail Rule #7: Establish and Enforce Rules of Online
   Etiquette   38

**Chapter 8: Special Netiquette Considerations for
Managers**
E-Mail Rule #8: Apply E-Mail Rules
   Consistently—from Summer Interns to the CEO   45

Chapter 9: LISTSERV® Policy
E-Mail Rule #9: Impose Policies and Procedures to
   Control LISTSERV Participation and Content   49

Chapter 10: Corporate Road Warriors
E-Mail Rule #10: Don't Leave Home Without E-Mail
   Policies and Procedures   52

Chapter 11: Failure to Establish or Enforce Policy
E-Mail Rule #11: Rules Exist for Businesses That
   Want to Remain in Business   55

PART THREE
Retaining E-Mail Business Records   61

**Chapter 12: Retaining Business Records: The
Legal Foundation for E-Mail Management**
E-Mail Rule #12: Treat E-Mail as a Business Record   63

Chapter 13: E-Mail Business Record Retention
E-Mail Rule #13: Retain Business Record E-Mail
   According to Written and Enforced Retention Rules   70

Chapter 14: Developing Retention Rules
E-Mail Rule #14: Apply Retention Principles to
   E-Mail Records   76

Chapter 15: SEC and NASD Regulations
E-Mail Rule #15: E-Mail Retention Periods May Be
Determined by Regulatory Bodies 79

Chapter 16: Record Retention Versus Backup Tapes or Stored E-Mail
E-Mail Rule #16: Don't Be Set Up by Backup 81

Chapter 17: Software Solutions
E-Mail Rule #17: E-Mail Rules Apply to Automation,
Too 89

Chapter 18: Outsourcing E-Mail Storage and Retention
E-Mail Rule #18: Assess the Legal and Business
Ramifications Before Moving E-Mail Off Site 93

Chapter 19: Educating Employees About E-Mail Retention
E-Mail Rule #19: Make E-Mail Retention Simple for
Employees 98

PART FOUR
E-Mail Business Records as Legal Evidence 105

Chapter 20: E-Mail Business Records as Legal Evidence
E-Mail Rule #20: Prepare to Produce E-Mail for
Audits, Investigations, or Lawsuits 107

Chapter 21: Records Management
E-Mail Rule #21: Manage E-Mail Business Records to
Ensure Accuracy and Trustworthiness 117

Chapter 22: E-Mail Discovery
E-Mail Rule #22: Manage E-Mail in Anticipation of
Litigation, Audits, and Investigations 122

Chapter 23: Destruction of Evidence
E-Mail Rule #23: It's Illegal to Destroy E-Mail
Evidence After You Have Received Notice of a
Lawsuit or During a Trial 135

Chapter 24: Discovery Rules for Employees
E-Mail Rule #24: E-Discovery Is Inevitable—Be
   Prepared   139

Chapter 25: Creating an E-Discovery Response Strategy
E-Mail Rule #25: Plan Today to Meet the Challenges
   of Litigation, Audits, and Investigations Tomorrow   142

PART FIVE
E-Mail Security   147

Chapter 26: E-Mail Security
E-Mail Rule #26: Develop Policies and Procedures to
   Secure E-Mail   149

Chapter 27: Physical and Network Security
E-Mail Rule #27: Strategic E-Mail Security Involves
   Physical and Network Security   157

Chapter 28: Content Security—Inbound
E-Mail Rule #28: Inbound Message and Attachment
   Content Is Critical to E-Mail Security   162

Chapter 29: Content Security—Outbound
E-Mail Rule #29: Outbound E-Mail Is Critical to
   E-Mail Security   168

Chapter 30: E-Mail System Security
E-Mail Rule #30: Develop Policies and Procedures to
   Ensure That Your E-Mail System Is Secure   173

Chapter 31: Spam
E-Mail Rule #31: Address the Sending, Forwarding,
   and Receiving of Spam in Your E-Mail Policy   179

PART SIX
Mixed Messages: Managing Alternative Communications Technologies   185

Chapter 32: Instant Messaging
E-Mail Rule #32: Retain and Manage Business
   Records Created by Alternative Communications
   Technologies   187

Chapter 33: Other Communications Technologies
E-Mail Rule #33: Establish E-Rules and Training for
Alternative Technologies 192

**Chapter 34: Peer-to-Peer File Networking
Technology**
E-Mail Rule #34: Combine Employee Rules with
Network Administration Techniques to Limit Risks 198

Chapter 35: E-Mail Variations
E-Mail Rule #35: Apply E-Mail Rules to
Nontraditional Use and Technologies 202

PART SEVEN
Employee Education 205

**Chapter 36: Training Is Key to E-Risk
Management Success**
E-Mail Rule #36: Train, Train, Train . . . Then Train
Some More 207

**Chapter 37: Instilling a Sense of Ownership in
Employees**
E-Mail Rule #37: Employee Compliance Is Key to
E-Risk Management Success 212

Notes 217

Appendixes 225

Index 249

About the Authors 255

Preface

This book is designed to provide guidelines for reducing work-place liabilities and managing e-mail and other data communications. *E-Mail Rules* is sold as a general overview and guide and does not provide legal advice or a legal opinion on any topic contained within.

The authors of *E-Mail Rules* did not and could not contemplate every situation, problem, or issue that may arise when using e-mail or other communications technology. This book does not purport to be exhaustive of all situations that may arise when using, implementing, or relying on such technologies.

Before taking any action on any matter addressed in *E-Mail Rules*, readers should consult with and be guided by professionals competent to address legal, regulatory, human resources, technology, compliance, policy, and other issues.

Specific institutions or industries may be required to follow different or additional rules from those described in *E-Mail Rules*. Before taking any action, consult a professional for advice regarding the specific laws, regulations, and rules governing your industry. The policies, rules, directives, and sample language contained in *E-Mail Rules* are provided as examples and are for illustrative purposes only. They are not exhaustive, complete, or appropriate for all institutions or situations. Such policies, rules, directives, or sample language should be followed only after receiving competent legal or other professional advice. Depending on the industry, circumstance, or regulatory or legal realities, the policies, rules, directives, and sample language contained in *E-Mail Rules* may not be adequate, sufficient, or appropriate.

Acknowledgments

The authors extend sincere thanks to those who generously contributed encouragement and support, expertise and information to help make this book possible. Most notably, we are grateful to our corporate sponsors, partners, and friends: Chris Witeck and the marketing team at Clearswift; Peter Delle Donne and Margaret Rimmler of Iron Mountain and the Digital Archives of Iron Mountain; and Amena Ali, Jocelyn Johnson, and Chris Gray of Legato Systems, Inc.

Nancy Flynn thanks her research assistant, Diana Cely, for her on-target and on-time efforts. She also thanks Paul Schodorf for his unwavering support and clear-headed advice.

Randy Kahn is particularly grateful for the substantial contribution and input of Barclay Blair of Kahn Consulting, Inc. Without Barclay's assistance this book would not be as insightful or technically in-depth. Sincere thanks to Diane Silverberg of Kovitz Shifrin Nesbit for her input. He also gives special thanks to his wife, Melissa, and his children, Dylan, Lily, and Teddy. Without their love, understanding, and encouragement, this book would not have been possible. Randy would also like to thank his father, Ted Kahn, for his support and inspiration.

Finally, a special thank-you to literary agent Sheree Bykofsky and AMACOM acquisitions editor Jacqueline Flynn for their belief in this book and help in making it happen.

PART ONE
The Case for E-Mail Management

CHAPTER 1

Introduction
E-Mail Rule #1: Strategic E-Mail Management Reduces Liabilities

Whether you employ one part-time worker or 100,000 full-time professionals, any time you allow employees access to your e-mail system, you put your organization's assets, future, and reputation at risk. Regardless of industry type, company size, or status as a for-profit or not-for-profit entity, the accidental misuse and intentional abuse of e-mail by employees can (and all too often does) create million-dollar (and occasionally billion-dollar) headaches for employers.

From lawsuits to laptop theft to lost productivity, workplace e-risks abound. Fully 78 percent of employers report employees abusing e-mail and the Internet.[1] In recent years, highly publicized cases of e-mail abuse and misuse have involved household names including Arthur Anderson,[2] the *New York Times*,[3] Xerox,[4] and numerous U.S. state and federal government agencies.

It's not just inexperienced staff and vengeful employees who are creating electronic liabilities. Hardly a week goes by without at least one CEO, CFO, stockbroker, or lawyer (experienced managers and skilled professionals who should know better) making newsworthy e-mail gaffes that trigger everything from tumbling stock prices to congressional investigations to media feeding frenzies.

Cautionary tales for employers, these high-profile e-disaster stories barely scratch the surface of the potential legal and business liabilities related to e-mail misuse and abuse. Whether sent by the chairman of the board or a summer intern, an ill-conceived or inappropriate e-mail message can savage your organization's financial resources, talent pool, investment rating, and public profile.

Fortunately for savvy employers committed to ending e-mail abuse and reducing electronic risk, there is a solution. By developing and implementing the type of comprehensive, strategic e-mail management program detailed in *E-Mail Rules*, employers can anticipate e-mail disasters, address employee misuse, derail intentional abuse, curtail e-mail blunders, and limit costly electronic liabilities.

Take a Holistic Approach to E-Mail Management

Despite the broad scope of electronic business risks and legal liability, most organizations to date have focused solely on the most obvious forms of e-mail abuse—with sexual content, pornographic images, and offensive jokes topping the list. Management angst over adults-only e-mail is reflected in the fact that more than 46 percent of U.S. employers have disciplined or terminated employees for sending sexually suggestive or explicit material via the office e-mail system.[5]

While employers are to be commended for their efforts to keep e-mail content clean, the current level of e-risk management falls far short of the goal of maximizing the business and legal value and overall effectiveness of workplace e-mail. Organizations operating in the age of e-mail and the Internet need to adopt a more holistic approach to e-mail management.

Focusing on the rules of e-mail management, rather than on liability concerns alone, *E-Mail Rules* was written to help employers harness the power of e-mail and other digital communication tools. By adhering to the rules of e-mail, organizations work faster, more efficiently, and in a legally sound manner. To that end, employers are advised to anticipate and address the challenges stemming from four primary types of e-mail abuse:

1. **Intentional misconduct explicitly designed to harm employers and devastate e-mail systems.** Topping this list is the theft of proprietary information. A popular form of intentional misconduct among cyberthieves and e-saboteurs, confidential data theft is big business, accounting for more than $170 million in financial losses in 2002.[6]

   Other examples of devastating e-mail misconduct include attacking e-mail systems, flooding e-mail systems with large attachments packed with restricted content, and sharing passwords with competitors, hackers, and other unauthorized persons.

2. **Intentional misconduct that causes peripheral harm.** Employees who send harassing e-mail messages to coworkers fall into this camp. While the sender may not intend to trigger a workplace lawsuit that costs the organization time, money, and credibility, employers nonetheless are put at risk. Yet, in spite of the potential cost, only 28 percent of employers have disciplined or terminated employees for sending menacing, harassing, discriminatory, or otherwise objectionable e-mail.[7]

   Another example of intentional, but by no means devastating, conduct involves wasting company resources by making excessive personal use of the organization's e-mail system. While the user's motive may be nothing more than a love of shopping or a love affair (rather than revenge, fraud, or theft), the organization nonetheless faces potential damages in the form of lost productivity, legal fees, and settlement costs. In fact, financial losses related to this type of abuse soared from $35 million in 2001 to more than $50 million 12 months later, according to the 2002 CSI/FBI Computer Crime and Security Survey.[8]

3. **Inadvertent acts, foolish accidents, and miscues.** When it comes to e-mail, accidents and miscues can cause just as much damage as intentional abuse. Should an employee accidentally hit "reply all" instead of "reply," for example, sensitive company information may be lost, right along with employee productivity and bandwidth. If an employee walks away from a live e-mail account for ten minutes, that may be all the time a rogue employee needs to do serious

damage to, or from, your e-mail system. If you think you're
immune to security breaches, accidental or intentional,
think again. Ninety percent of large corporations and government agencies suffered computer security breaches in
2002, with 80 percent reporting financial losses as a result.[9]

4. **Oversight.** Occurring primarily at the system level and
often stemming from ignorance of potential risks, oversight
occurs when an e-mail system has been incorrectly configured or poorly maintained. Failure to install the most current security patches or to protect the e-mail server from
outsiders, for example, is a common form of oversight.

E-Mail Management Is the Application of Fundamental *E-Mail Rules*

E-Mail Rules is intended as a best practices tool kit for business
people confused by and concerned about how to manage their
e-mail, what electronic records to retain or delete, how to maximize the effectiveness of their organizations' e-mail systems, and
other workplace e-mail and legal liability issues. Among the
E-Mail Rules detailed in these pages are:

■ **Retention: You Can't Just Throw It Away.** Organizations
rely on e-mail as a critical business tool. With this reliance
comes the obligation to treat information contained in e-mail
systems as assets to be managed and protected. The first step:
creating retention rules based on current law and sound business judgment. *E-Mail Rules* provides effective retention rules
to protect organizations' assets and futures by ensuring e-mail
needed for legal and business purposes is retained, while nonrecord and administrative e-mail is properly disposed of when no
longer needed.

■ **Disposition: You Can't Keep Everything Forever.** What to
retain? Some organizations mistakenly believe e-mail management simply means disposing of everything after 30, 60, or 90
days, regardless of content. Other companies retain all e-mail
forever. Neither approach is ideal. While retention of some

e-mail is required for legal and business purposes, retaining all e-mail is neither cost effective nor efficient.

E-Mail Rules offers guidelines for disposing of records in accordance with written retention policy. E-mail efficiency is promoted, while the organization is shielded from allegations that records were destroyed following the initiation of a lawsuit, audit, or investigation.

▓ **Classification: E-Mail Is Intended for Business Purposes.** E-mail often contains confidential documents, trade secrets, transaction details, and other critical information that must be managed as business assets. However, e-mail also is used by many to book lunch appointments and conduct other personal and quasi-business activities. Organizations need to develop and implement classification rules to evaluate and address messages based on content.

▓ **Transmission: E-Mail Interception Is a Risk.** Where an e-mail is sent may be just as important as what it contains. *E-Mail Rules* addresses the establishment of transmission rules that consider the vulnerability of the environment through which messages are sent. For example, transmission rules might allow the use of a secure Intranet system to send confidential documents but ban transmission outside a corporate firewall via the unprotected Internet.

▓ **Data Protection: Failure to Control Business-Critical Data Is Not an Option.** Unless organizations establish enterprise-wide rules for e-mail management, they are at risk of exposing and losing business-critical data. *E-Mail Rules* shows employers how technology, policy, and employee training can work together to dramatically minimize the exposure of their business-critical data.

▓ **Central Management: Necessary in the Age of E-Mail.** Although economic forces, corporate culture, and technological architectures have promoted the development of distributed organizations, corporate information and records must still be managed centrally. *E-Mail Rules* offers guidelines for central management, adding evidentiary value to records, increasing access, and decreasing the expense of record retrieval and reproduction. Employers learn how to manage critical information by corralling messaging records no matter where they are created and stored.

■ **Metadata: Information About E-Mail Is Critical.** An e-mail message without metadata (the data that manages the data) has limited evidentiary value. Consequently, organizations must develop rules to capture the who, what, when, and where of e-mail if messages are to have legal or business value as records.

■ **Technological Solutions: Is the Answer Only a Purchase Order Away?** Software manufacturers, having identified the management conundrum created by e-mail, offer technological solutions to e-mail challenges. Effective e-mail management calls for the development of management policies first, followed by the installation of technology to help implement policies. Approaching the problem in reverse order, as many organizations do, results in management policies that don't truly reflect or address the organization's needs.

■ **User Management: Take Control of the Desktop.** E-mail systems are increasingly feature rich, providing users with an ever-expanding range of options for the creation, transmission, and management of e-mail from their desktops. However, many of these features conspire to limit organizational management of e-mail. *E-Mail Rules* helps readers sort through the options and make informed decisions.

■ **Electronic Time Management: Sending, Receiving, Replying, and Deleting—While Still Putting in a Productive Day.** The average U.S. worker spends up to four hours a day sending and receiving e-mail,[10] creating a time management nightmare for executives and employees. *E-Mail Rules* offers tips and techniques, from the development and implementation of e-mail policy to the establishment of netiquette rules, to the creation of corporate content guidelines, designed to streamline the creation, forwarding, reading, and replying process.

■ **Mixed Messages: It's Not Just E-Mail Anymore.** Instant Messaging and other technologies combining text, voice, and video are entering the corporate mainstream. Messages are sent and received on a dizzying array of portable devices that seem to evade traditional approaches to methodical records retention and management. *E-Mail Rules* helps organizations implement these new technologies while balancing user efficiency with e-mail records management.

Self-Assessment: Understanding Your Organization's Risks and E-Mail Management Needs

Where do you stand when it comes to e-risk and e-mail management? Does your organization's incoming and outgoing e-mail constitute a business record? Do you even know the difference between a valuable business record and insignificant data?

Complete the following self-assessment to determine your awareness of organizational liabilities and the *E-Mail Rules* that can help reduce your risks, enhance employee productivity, and protect your organization's future.

1. Do your employees use e-mail to negotiate, enter into, or maintain business relationships with clients, customers, vendors, or service providers? __ Yes __ No

2. Is e-mail used regularly by your staff to communicate with customers or clients? __ Yes __ No

3. Are spreadsheets, word processing documents, and other business-related content routinely incorporated into or attached to e-mail by employees? __ Yes __ No

4. Do employees communicate with executives, supervisors, or the human resources department via e-mail? __ Yes __ No

5. Do employees purchase services or products on behalf of the organization via e-mail? __ Yes __ No

6. Does the organization communicate with lawyers or accountants via e-mail? __ Yes __ No

7. Does the organization use e-mail to receive or transmit business-related complaints, recommendations, problems, questions, or inquiries?   __ Yes __ No

8. Is internal e-mail used to communicate information about product development, sales, service offerings, customer service, marketing, or advertising?   __ Yes __ No

9. Does your organization have a written e-mail policy governing employees' e-mail usage?   __ Yes __ No

10. Does your organization conduct ongoing employee education related to e-mail policy and procedures, business record retention, and security?   __ Yes __ No

What Your Responses Mean

If you answered yes to the first eight questions, many of your organization's incoming and outgoing e-mails likely constitute business records. From a legal perspective, the process of formally defining, properly identifying, and effectively retaining business records is the single most important e-mail challenge facing business today.

A *yes* response to question nine places you in the majority. More than 81 percent of large employers have written policies governing employee e-mail use. The problem is that fewer than 24 percent of organizations support e-mail policy with employee training.[11] Don't leave employee compliance to chance. See Parts 2 and 7, respectively, for guidelines on the development of effective e-mail policy and the establishment of continuing education in support of your organization's strategic e-mail management program.

E-Mail Rules Is the Ultimate Reference Guide for Managing E-Mail

Whether your concern is e-mail business record retention and deletion, e-mail policy and procedures, legal liability and document discovery, technological tools or security snafus, *E-Mail Rules* has you covered.

By applying the tips, techniques, and tools found in *E-Mail Rules*, employers can develop and maintain customized, strategic e-mail management programs designed to successfully reduce electronic liabilities, increase employee productivity, and protect corporate assets.

Recap and E-Action Plan

E-Mail Rule #1: Strategic E-Mail Management Reduces Liabilities

1. Any time you allow employees access to your e-mail system, you potentially put your organization at risk.

2. Implement a strategic e-risk management program to help control liabilities.

3. Adopt a holistic approach to e-mail management.

4. Apply e-mail rules that address intentional misconduct, accidents, and oversight.

5. Retention rules are critical—the greatest legal and business challenge facing employers today.

CHAPTER 2

Real-World Legal Issues

E-Mail Rule #2: Manage Employees' E-Mail Use

You've seen the headlines. Whether "Fifty Employees Fired for E-Mail Abuse" or "Pornographic Images Found in State Agency's E-Mail System," the story is the same. Employees' accidental misuse or intentional abuse of e-mail systems has led to e-disaster, costing employers time, money, and credibility as the news media rush to cover salacious stories on otherwise dry news days.

How pervasive is e-mail abuse in the workplace? Common enough that nearly 47 percent of large U.S. employers review e-mail messages, with 63 percent monitoring Internet connections. Fear of lawsuits is the number-one reason for employers' concern, with 68 percent of organizations citing legal liability as the primary reason to monitor employees' electronic communications. Not surprising, given that nearly 10 percent of employers have received subpoenas for employee e-mail and another 10 percent have defended sexual/racial harassment/discrimination claims based on employee e-mail and Internet use.[1]

Mindful of legal, productivity, security, and other electronic risks, more than 81 percent of employers have established written e-mail policies designed to guide employees' online activity and control content.[2] Unfortunately, while written e-mail policy forms the foundation of an effective e-mail program, it cannot stand alone in the battle against workplace e-risks. On the contrary, it takes a comprehensive understanding of technological and legal issues, combined with written policy and formal training, to successfully battle intentional and inadvertent e-mail system abuse.

Self-Assessment: Is E-Mail a Source of Unmanaged Liability in Your Organization?

1. Are employees allowed remote access to the organization's e-mail system? __ Yes __ No

2. Do employees use e-mail to document business events, activities, or transactions? __ Yes __ No

3. Do employees use laptops or handheld computers to transmit e-mail? __ Yes __ No

4. Is confidential data secured when road warriors travel with laptops or PDAs? __ Yes __ No

5. Are employees permitted to shop or trade stocks online during the lunch hour and other breaks? __ Yes __ No

6. Has an employee ever reported a lost, misplaced, or stolen laptop computer? __ Yes __ No

7. Does the organization retain copies of all business e-mail? __ Yes __ No

8. Does the organization restrict employees' personal use of company-owned laptops? __ Yes __ No

9. Does the organization have a policy governing online group discussions? __ Yes __ No

10. Are you aware of employees violating company e-mail policy? __ Yes __ No

11. Can you locate and access old e-mail whenever you need it? __ Yes __ No

12. Do the organization's in-house lawyers
        communicate with employees via e-mail?   ___ **Yes** ___ **No**

What Your Responses Mean

If employees are using e-mail to conduct business, communicate with friends, and engage in other personal business (on site or away from the office), the mix of professional and personal messages creates potential risks. If your company lawyer sends privileged e-mail messages, or executives leave the office with laptop and handheld computers laden with confidential information, a whole new set of potentially costly risks arises. Finally, if you are conducting business via e-mail, and you can't locate messages documenting transactions and events, you have a problem. Manage your electronic liabilities today or risk e-disaster tomorrow.

Beyond Naked Pictures: A Methodology for E-Risk Management

While the improper use of your organization's information system may waste valuable financial and human resources, it is the misuse of e-mail in particular that creates liability. Whether triggered by offensive messages, lost productivity, or security breaches, inappropriate online behavior is bad for business and has an enormous potential legal impact on your organization.

Take a Strategic Approach to Electronic Risk Management

Before drafting e-mail policy and implementing risk management procedures, be sure you have a clear and accurate picture of your organization's e-mail and legal risks. Your strategic planning efforts should include: (1) determining and focusing on the specific legal and risk issues that are likely to impact your organization; and (2) categorizing potentially problematic conduct. As detailed in the Introduction, those categories include intentional misconduct explicitly designed to harm the organization and its e-mail system; intentional misconduct that causes only peripheral harm; inadvertent acts, foolish accidents, and miscues; and oversight.

Forming Your E-Risk Management Team[3]

Regardless of whether you operate a large organization with a full-time staff of in-house experts, or a small business that relies on part-time help and the advice of paid consultants, you will want to form a working team to oversee the development and implementation of your strategic e-risk management plan and the e-mail policies and procedures that grow out of your research.

The size of your team will depend on the size of your organization, the scope of your electronic exposure, and your willingness to commit financial and human resources to e-risk management. For most organizations, the team will be made up of some or all of the following professionals:

1. **Senior company official.** Increase the likelihood of success by appointing a senior executive to oversee your e-risk management team. The involvement of a top executive will signal to the staff that your organization is fully committed to e-risk management. With the right champion leading the charge, your e-risk management team should have no trouble receiving necessary funding and support.

2. **Legal counsel.** Legal and regulatory compliance is key to successful e-risk management. Have your legal counsel review organizational risks, employee rights, and employer responsibilities. Involve your lawyer in policy development to ensure that all applicable federal and state laws and regulations are addressed. If you operate facilities overseas, be sure the e-mail-related laws and regulations of each country are reflected in written policies.

3. **Human resources manager.** Involve your HR manager in all aspects of e-risk management, from research and planning, through policy writing, to employee education and enforcement.

4. **Chief information officer.** Your chief information officer (CIO) can help bridge the gap between people problems

and technical solutions. Information management professionals can play an important role in identifying electronic
risks and recommending the most effective technologies to
help manage those risks.

5. **Computer security expert.** While developing your e-risk
   management and e-mail policy program, take time to assess
   and address your organization's computer security capabilities and challenges. If you don't employ an in-house computer security professional, hire an outside consultant to
   assess and address your security risks.

6. **Training specialist.** E-mail rules, policies, and procedures
   are only as good as your employees' willingness to adhere
   to them. Spend at least as much time communicating your
   e-mail policies as you do developing them. Don't rely on
   employees to train themselves. Support initial policy training with continuing education tools and programs designed
   to keep employees' electronic communications clean, clear,
   and compliant.

Focusing Your E-Risk Management Team

You must gain a comprehensive understanding of employees'
e-mail activity and associated risks before making determina-
tions about conduct and policy guidelines. The types of activity
your e-risk management team will want to assess and address
include:

Intentional Conduct: Shopping for a Bundle of Risks Online

Online shopping during the lunch hour is an intentional act that
may impact the shopper's productivity, overwhelm the mail
room as packages arrive (a widely reported business concern),
or drag the organization into a dispute if the shopper fails to pay
for merchandise purchased via the organization's e-mail system.
Without thoroughly evaluating the act and potential harm,
management cannot be certain whether online shopping should
be permitted or outlawed. By carefully evaluating conduct and
risks, the organization may be able to arrive at a solution that
allows online shopping while mitigating risks.

Intentional Conduct: Customer Service May Equal Organizational Disservice

Let's say a pharmaceutical manufacturer is considering allowing customers to submit complaints via e-mail or Instant Messaging. Ease and speed are touted as benefits. But what happens if, thanks to poor record keeping, the manufacturer cannot turn over customer complaints to the Food and Drug Administration if requested to do so? An intentional act that initially seemed harmless, the process of submitting complaints via e-mail, may need to be disallowed because of potential regulatory problems. Had the organization not taken time to evaluate e-mail policies and procedures from a legal and compliance standpoint, the process may have been allowed, and the company would have been at risk.

Inadvertent Acts: Faster Is Not Always Better

To speed processing, the claims department is eager to transmit medical claims for processing via e-mail. But what happens if confidential medical records are accidentally addressed and sent to unauthorized persons? The solution may involve hands-on management, encryption, or requiring employees to send a confirming e-mail test message, followed by the sensitive information.

Oversight: Who's Really Reading and Writing the Bosses' E-Mail?

According to an online poll conducted by the International Association of Administrative Professionals (IAAP) and The ePolicy Institute, 43 percent of administrative assistants ghostwrite e-mail responses under their bosses' names. Another 26 percent screen executives' incoming e-mail, and 29 percent are authorized to delete e-mail addressed to the executive.[4]

Problems may loom for organizations whose e-mail accounts are equipped with digitized signing capabilities. The same password that opens executives' e-mail accounts also accesses their digitized signatures. Without an understanding of the technology, misuse of executives' signatures is a real risk.

Employers Can Be Responsible for Employees' Wrongs

Fair or not, an organization may be held responsible for the misconduct of its employees. Known as vicarious liability (and the related legal concept of *respondeat superior*), this legal principle would come into play if an employee filed a discrimination claim based on an offensive e-mail message sent by another employee.

Organizations are at greatest risk when they fail to protect employees from offensive conduct. Fortunately, if an employer makes reasonable efforts—through e-mail policy development and employee training—to prevent a hostile work environment, the bad acts of individual employees may not be attributable to the employer. In fact, the U.S. Supreme Court has made it clear that, through the development and enforcement of comprehensive policies, an organization can create a defense against sexual harassment or hostile work environment liabilities.[5]

Bottom line: Organizations that take time to develop strategic risk management programs, complete with written policy, employee training, and consistent enforcement, may have a viable defense against vicarious liability claims.

Self-Assessment: Anticipating and Addressing Intentional Misconduct, Inadvertent Acts, and Oversight

Scenario: You are a member of an e-risk management team that's developing e-mail rules to limit liability. Should you implement rules governing the following?

1. Forwarding e-mail to an external e-mail account. __ Yes __ No

2. Sending birthday cards to family members via office e-mail. __ Yes __ No

3. Designating all business e-mail as privileged and confidential. __ Yes __ No

4. Limiting online purchases to the lunch hour. __ Yes __ No

5. Using personal handheld computers to communicate with customers while employees are vacationing. ___ Yes ___ No

6. Participating in a recreational LIST-SERV® via the organization's e-mail system. ___ Yes ___ No

7. Sending free electronic greeting cards to coworkers via the organization's e-mail system. ___ Yes ___ No

8. Sending coworkers e-calendars featuring female and male swimsuit models. ___ Yes ___ No

9. Giving administrative assistants access to all employees' e-mail accounts, so messages may be checked during vacations and absences. ___ Yes ___ No

10. Allowing employees to e-mail nonreligious inspirational messages to colleagues. ___ Yes ___ No

What Your Responses Mean

Because employee e-mail conduct should be regulated, your organization may need to enact rules addressing many (or all) of these situations. Remember, seemingly tame or harmless behavior may trigger liability. So craft your rules carefully.

Recap and E-Action Plan

E-Mail Rule #2: Manage Employees' E-Mail Use

1. Improper e-mail use creates liabilities.

2. Assign a team to oversee development of your strategic e-risk management program.

3. Understand employees' e-mail activity and related risks before forming conduct rules and policy guidelines.

4. Employers may be held responsible for employees' wrongs.

5. Policy and training create a defense against vicarious liability.

CHAPTER 3

E-Mail Ownership and Cybertheft
E-Mail Rule #3: E-Mail Belongs to the Employer, Not the Employee

As detailed in Part 2, employers should use written e-mail policy to notify employees that e-mail messages, electronic documents, and computer passwords belong to the organization, not the individual. Stress the fact that theft of company records is a serious offense carrying possible civil or criminal penalties. If you are among the 47 percent of employers who monitor e-mail to thwart theft and other disasters,[1] take this opportunity to let your staff know.

Theft of Proprietary Information

In the paper world, employers rarely had to worry about disgruntled or vengeful employees driving to off-site record storage facilities and loading confidential information into their cars. It was just too risky and difficult to warrant an attempt.

In the age of e-mail, however, just about any document can be attached to e-mail and sent outside the organization. The problem is so pervasive that 20 percent of employers reported the theft of proprietary information in 2002, with losses totaling $171 million.[2]

Easy and largely undetected access makes data theft a growing concern for business. The transmission is completed instantly, and data remains intact inside the company. A recent survey finds one in ten employees has received confidential information via e-mail. A whopping 79 percent of employees admit to using e-mail to share confidential information with others—innocently or otherwise.[3]

No Organization Is Immune from Data Theft

Imagine that an unhappy employee is planning to leave your organization. In anticipation, the employee has been busy e-mailing work-related files to a home computer. The stolen files include a few embarrassing e-mails written by the boss, along with a confidential client list. The employee plans to use the material as leverage in case management fails to offer severance or opts to enforce its restrictive employment contract.

Corporate Espionage on the Rise

To help counter corporate espionage and theft of trade secrets, the government of the United States in 1996 enacted the Economic Espionage Act (EEA). The U.S. Department of Justice (DOJ) even maintains a Web site (www.cybercrime.gov/eeapub-.htm) on which it posts cases involving trade secret theft by U.S. citizens and corporations, as well as unauthorized use of computer systems.

While it's true that economic espionage and cybercrime cases often involve competitors or spies operating on behalf of domestic and foreign corporations or governments, the DOJ's site clearly illustrates the fact that insiders, greedy or disgruntled employees and ex-employees, are actively involved in data theft.

For example, take the case of Jeffrey W. Dorn, who used information from the employee placement firm he worked for to place a candidate on his own, for which he was paid directly. Dorn pled guilty to "one count of theft of a trade secret" and was ordered to pay restitution of $15,920 to his former employer. Dorn faces a maximum sentence of ten years in prison without parole.[4]

On a larger scale, in December 2001, Mikahel K. Chang was sentenced to one year and a day in prison, plus three years of supervised release, for theft of trade secrets from his former

California-based employer. Chang admitted that he used customer and order databases stolen from his former employer to make sales on his own—selling $300,000 worth of goods and pocketing $60,000 in profits in the process. To put his theft in context, his former employer stated that "his company would have been put out of business" if the databases had not been recovered by law enforcement.[5]

Authorization and Authenticity

New technologies always bring new opportunities for employee misuse and abuse. Strive to anticipate and address challenges by developing and instituting rules before new technology is deployed.

Scenario: A CEO who was tired of affixing handwritten signatures to business-related documents empowered an administrative assistant to add his digitized signature to official e-mail.

All went well until another employee abruptly quit, and security determined that the ex-employee had used the organization's e-mail system to purchase luxury items under the CEO's electronic signature. Both the company and the CEO were impacted by the former employee's illegal acts.

Ban Unauthorized Transactions

Put controls in place to block unauthorized e-mail transactions. In this case, had the CEO's e-mail account not been left active, the thief would have had to download the CEO's signature to another e-mail account. That might have caused the recipient to doubt the authenticity of the communication, in spite of the presence of the CEO's signature. Instruct employees and executives to exit e-mail accounts if they plan to be absent for more than a few minutes. Or have the IT department install software to automatically "time out" e-mail accounts after a short period of time.

With better controls on the use of the CEO's e-signature, which was unprotected on the computer workstations of both the CEO and the administrative assistant, perhaps the unauthorized transaction could have been avoided.

Sample Record Ownership Statement

Any record including e-mail messages you create, receive, and/ or use in the course of business is company property, which does not belong to you, other employees, or any third parties. At management's request, employees must make available any and all company records at any time, for any reason. When terminated voluntarily or involuntarily, employees must turn over originals (if available) and all copies (paper or electronic) of company records and e-mail messages to management. Any third parties working on behalf of the company must return the original and all copies of company records on request or at the termination of their contract with the company.

All records located in a company facility or facilities managed by outside entities on behalf of the company are presumed to be company property. All records created or stored on the company computer, e-mail servers, imaging system, communications system, telecommunication system, storage device, storage medium, or any other company system, medium, or device are presumed to be company property. All records that in any way pertain to the company or our business, no matter where they are located, are presumed to be company property, even if in the possession of a nonemployee or an entity other than the company.

Recap and E-Action Plan

E-Mail Rule #3: E-Mail Belongs to the Employer, Not the Employee

E-mail provides a multitude of unique opportunities for intentional and inadvertent misuse and abuse. While there is no completely foolproof way to prevent employee data theft, management can take steps to reduce its likelihood:

1. Monitor and review large e-mail attachments.

2. Advise employees that e-mail and other paper and electronic business records are the property of the organization.

3. Address e-mail ownership and confidentiality in your written e-mail policy.

4. Require employees to sign and date a written policy, acknowledging that e-mail and other paper and electronic business records belong to the organization.

5. Explain that theft of proprietary information may result in an employee's termination and may be punishable by civil or criminal penalties.

PART TWO

Designing and Implementing Effective E-Mail Policies

CHAPTER 4

Why Implement E-Mail Policies?

E-Mail Rule #4: E-Mail Can Come Back to Haunt You

Although most U.S.-based organizations rely on e-mail to run their businesses, not all have established policies, procedures, and rules similar to those applied to paper-based processes and other information systems.

Large institutions, for instance, typically have policies and rules regarding workplace conduct but fail to extend these rules to the creation and transmission of e-mail. Behind that oversight lurks potential long-term damage.

Content rules help keep e-mail free of personal opinions, off-color jokes, and inappropriate commentary, which can haunt organizations during litigation, audits, or other formal proceedings. Take the case of the large consulting firm sued by a client for inadequate performance. During the trial, damaging internal e-mail messages undercut the firm's defense. In one message, a consulting firm employee expressed the opinion that one of the consultants in question "should be taking community college courses, not billing for this."[1] Had management established and enforced policy banning personal opinions or commentary critical of the firm and its employees, it is unlikely that damning messages like this ever would have been written.

E-Mail as Legal Evidence

One of the ways in which e-mail is entered into evidence in court is to have it classified as a business record that satisfies the "Business Records Exception to the Hearsay Rule" (see below).

Normally, when hearing evidence in a case, the courts require direct testimony from individuals who witnessed or had firsthand knowledge of events. Their testimony is considered more accurate and trustworthy than hearsay evidence from those who simply recount what others said.

On their own, business records can be considered a form of hearsay and be excluded. Mindful that business records are an important source of evidence, however, the law long ago created an exception to the hearsay prohibition, the "Business Records Exception to the Hearsay Rule," which allows the admission of business records that are created and maintained in the ordinary course of business.

This rule recognizes the fact that corporations and government agencies typically continue to operate long after the creator of a given record is available to testify. It also acknowledges the financial and logistical nightmares litigants would face if forced to provide firsthand testimony for every document used in trial, especially when thousands of pages of evidence may be involved. Courts have admitted e-mail into evidence, but have excluded it as well.[2]

E-mail may be admitted into evidence for other reasons, too. E-mail that is considered a "Statement Against Interest" may be admitted, even if it fails to rise to the level of a business record. The courts' reasoning: If e-mail in your system contains a statement detrimental to your organization, it probably is true. After all, few of us are prone to documenting our self-criticism.

The bottom line: Fail to legitimize your e-mail system by applying business rules and establishing policy governing creation and content, and the courts may not consider your e-mail trustworthy and your messages as business records. You may not be able to use e-mail that is not a business record as evidence to support your case. But your opponent may be able to use your own e-mail against you as a "Statement Against Interest," if incriminating evidence is uncovered in your system.

Recap and E-Action Plan

E-Mail Rule #4: E-Mail Can Come Back to Haunt You

1. Content rules help keep e-mail clean of inappropriate and potentially damaging material.

2. Even though e-mail may be hearsay, it could still be used as evidence in court, if it were considered a business record.

3. Incriminating e-mail messages found in your system may be used against you during litigation.

CHAPTER 5

E-Mail Privacy
E-Mail Rule #5: There Is No One-Size-Fits-All E-Mail Policy

Not all e-mail policies are alike. This is especially true of employee privacy policies. Privacy laws vary by jurisdiction and must be researched and monitored in conjunction with policy development.

Under U.S. federal law, management can use the organization's written e-mail policy to inform employees that their e-mail may be monitored, and they have no reasonable expectation of privacy when it comes to sending and receiving e-mail. However, a multinational corporation based in the United States might not be able to apply this policy to European, Asian, or Middle Eastern employees. The Supreme Court of France, for example, has ruled that monitoring employee e-mail is improper, even with a written policy giving employees notice that management may be reading electronically over their shoulders.

Before implementing domestic privacy policies abroad, have the lawyer(s) responsible for your international facilities review and, as necessary, adjust them to meet the regulatory, legal, and cultural needs of each country in which the organization operates.

Federal Law Protects Employers

When it comes to e-mail policy, employers are doing a good job with the basics. Fully 81 percent of large U.S. employers have established written e-mail policies. And eighty-four percent not only notify employees of the organization's legal right to monitor e-mail and Internet activity, they also stress that employees should not expect privacy when using the e-mail system.[1] The premise is that if employees know employers can and do review e-mail, then employees will be disinclined to misuse and abuse the system.

U.S. courts in general accept the fact that informed employees neither would nor should consider e-mail their own. In fact, even in situations in which employers have assured employees that their incoming and outgoing e-mail would not be monitored, the courts have ruled that employees nonetheless should not expect privacy when using a company-owned system.[2]

What the Future Holds

While courts interpreting the federal Electronic Communications Privacy Act (ECPA) have made it clear that a company accessing its own e-mail is acting within the terms of the law, bills are advanced regularly (most notably in California), seeking to clarify the fact that employee e-mail may not be accessed unless employees receive prior written notice in the form of an e-mail policy. Those bills have routinely been defeated, but that situation could change. To be safe, employers should assign their e-risk management team or legal counsel the task of monitoring legislation related to e-mail privacy on the state, federal, and, if appropriate, international levels.

Sample Privacy Statement

All records and e-mail that are created, stored, transmitted, or received using company resources (including but not limited to computers, telecommunications systems, e-mail servers, and fax machines) should be for business purposes only. The company reserves the right to access and review the content of any record, nonrecord, document, or e-mail message created, stored, transmitted, or received using company computers and/or other company-provided resources located in company facilities or on company property. Employees are not granted and should not expect any right to privacy with respect to such records, nonrecords, documents, or e-mail messages.

Recap and E-Action Plan
E-Mail Rule #5: There Is No One-Size-Fits-All E-Mail Policy

1. Make sure your e-mail policy establishes no expectations of privacy.

2. Review HR and other policies to ensure that your e-mail privacy statement conforms to the privacy statement that appears in other company policies.

3. Use your policy to inform employees that they should not expect privacy with regard to the organization's e-mail, computer, or telecommunications systems.

4. Research and conform policies to the relevant regulations and laws of the states and countries in which employees and offices are located.

5. Develop and maintain a list of excluded employees who are covered by laws in jurisdictions that prohibit review or monitoring of e-mail transmissions and on-line activities.

CHAPTER 6

E-Mail Content
E-Mail Rule #6: Control Risk by Controlling Content

Controlling Content to Control Risks[1]

One of the most effective ways for employers to reduce electronic risks is also one of the simplest. By requiring employees to use appropriate, businesslike language in e-mail and other electronic documents, employers can limit their liability risks and improve the overall effectiveness of the organization's e-communications in the process.

Language that is obscene, racist, discriminatory, menacing, harassing, or in any way offensive has no place in the workplace. Use written e-mail policy to ban language that could negatively affect your organization's business relationships, damage your corporate reputation, or trigger a lawsuit.

Real-Life E-Disaster Story:
Turning Off Customers Via E-Mail

After ordering a baby crib from an online furniture retailer, a new mother e-mailed the company's customer service department to express displeasure over slow delivery. Needless to say, the customer service department's reply was not the answer the buyer was hoping for.

> Dear Customer:
> We got your feedback on doing business with our company. Obviously you never read the attached note we sent you the day after we received your order!!!!
>
> Also, our site says we will process your order within 2–3 days of receiving it, not drop it at your door. Further, our order process confirmation says allow up to 5 business days in transit while in the hands of the ground transportation service.
>
> We did everything we said we would do for you. Problem is you do not read.
>
> Please do not return to us as a customer, since you are exactly the type we do not want.
>
> Our rating of you as a customer is: Ignorant and enjoys it.
>
> Sincerely,
> Customer Service

Imagine the impact this type of "customer service" would have on your organization's reputation and bottom line. Is it possible your employees are insulting, defaming, harassing, or otherwise offending customers and vendors via e-mail? Couple content rules with employee education to ensure that electronic communications (external and internal) are as clean and clear as they are safe and secure.

What Constitutes Appropriate Online Content?

Instruct employees to compose businesslike messages that are free of:

■ Jokes (many jokes are told at the expense of an individual or group of people and may be perceived as harassing, menacing, or defamatory)

■ Obscene language and sexual content

■ Racial comments

■ Harassing or menacing comments

- Negative or defamatory remarks

- Ethnic slurs

- Unsubstantiated opinions, rumors, and innuendoes

Sample Content Statement

Employees may not use the Company's e-mail system, network, or Internet/Intranet access for offensive or harassing statements or language, including disparagement of others based on their race, color, religion, national origin, veteran status, ancestry, disability, age, sex, or sexual orientation.

How to Handle Unsolicited Messages That Violate Policy

Use your written e-mail policy to instruct employees how to handle offensive messages that land in their e-mail inboxes unsolicited. Protect employees by instructing them to report unsolicited and offensive e-mail to the appropriate supervisor. Explain that deleting, replying to, or forwarding banned messages may put the employee in the loop—making an innocent recipient party to the violation.

Don't Take Chances with Content

If you have any doubt about your employees' willingness to adhere to the organization's e-mail policy and ban on inappropriate language, consider applying a technological solution to your people problem.

By installing content filtering software that works in concert with your e-mail policy and is programmed to detect and report employee use of banned language, you can stay on top of policy violations. As an added bonus, programming your monitoring software to track competitors' names along with inappropriate language may alert you to any electronic communication that is taking place between your employees and competitors, for example. What you don't know could hurt you. For instance, an employee could be planning to open a business or make a career move, courtesy of your customer lists, formulas, or other trade secrets.

Just be sure to put your policy into place before installing monitoring software. Remember: When you learn of employee misdeeds, you may have no choice but to take action. Failing to discipline employees for their misconduct may create liability as well. Your rules and policy should guide the technology, not the other way around.

Using Conversational Language

The most effective tone for electronic business correspondence is professional, yet conversational. How do you achieve that tone? Take the colleague, customer, and competitor test. Imagine you are in an elevator crowded with colleagues, customers, and competitors. What tone would you use? What would you say? What information would you reveal, and what would you keep under wraps? If you wouldn't say it aloud while sharing close quarters with the people you work for, with, and against, don't write it in an e-mail message.

For additional guidelines and information about cyberlanguage, see Nancy Flynn's book *The ePolicy Handbook: Designing and Implementing Effective E-Mail, Internet, and Software Policies.*[2]

Maintaining E-Mail's Contextual String

E-mail is a contextual medium. As such, the meaning of any given message is typically linked to one or more related messages. This characteristic makes e-mail a fast way to communicate, as a message often collects valuable information as it moves from one reader to the next. Unfortunately, speedy communication is not always safe and complete communication.

When an e-mail message is taken out of context and viewed in isolation, the sender's meaning may be misconstrued or misinterpreted. An e-mail reply, when read in isolation from the message that triggered the response, also may be misunderstood. Litigators regularly take advantage of e-mail's contextual challenges.

Imagine a manager sending an e-mail that reads, "Steve's team needs to have its draft to the committee by close of business today." Steve in turn shoots off this speedy reply: "I am all over Sue and Mary. Trust me; they will do what I say."

Taken out of context, Steve's reply could be used to demonstrate he is at best heavy handed and domineering. In the worst-case scenario, Steve might be perceived as unprofessional, with a discriminatory, hostile, or dismissive attitude toward female employees.

Be sure to address context in your e-mail policy. If there is any chance the meaning of a message will change materially if read in isolation from the message(s) that preceded it, instruct employees to attach all previous e-mail(s) to clear up any potential confusion.

Recap and E-Action Plan
E-Mail Rule #6: Control Risk by Controlling Content

1. One of the simplest, most effective ways to control risk is to control content.

2. Use your e-mail policy to ban language that is racist, sexist, obscene, menacing, harassing, discriminatory, or in any way objectionable or inappropriate.

3. Support your written e-mail policy with content filtering software.

4. Establish rules to ensure that the contextual string of e-mail is retained.

CHAPTER 7

Netiquette
E-Mail Rule #7: Establish and Enforce Rules of Online Etiquette

A Netiquette Primer for Employees[1]

The power of e-mail is considerable. With e-mail, you can send a message around the globe as quickly and conveniently as you can communicate with an office mate. You can distribute lengthy documents across time zones and continents with just a click of your mouse. And you can respond to a client's inquiry or a supervisor's request in a matter of seconds.

With all that power, however, comes responsibility. Every e-mail message sent by an employee reflects on the organization's credibility and the writer's professionalism. Electronic documents that are poorly constructed and riddled with mechanical errors can sink careers and turn off customers. E-mail messages inadvertently sent to the wrong recipient can compromise confidences, create hard feelings, and cause embarrassment. Electronic correspondence that is menacing, harassing, pornographic, or otherwise inappropriate can trigger litigation.

An effective e-mail policy should incorporate the rules of "netiquette," or e-mail etiquette. By addressing and enforcing netiquette rules, employers can help reduce the likelihood of employees writing and sending inappropriate messages that can trigger lawsuits and other risks.

Mind Your Electronic Manners

Use your e-mail policy to provide employees with basic guidelines for acceptable and effective electronic correspondence. By its nature, e-mail is a "cold" medium. Messages written and conversations held on screen lack the warmth of face-to-face discussions and telephone calls, which benefit, respectively, from body language and intonation.

Couple its coldness with the tendency of many writers to type messages quickly and in some cases thoughtlessly, and it is easy to see how e-mail can result in hurt feelings, misunderstandings, and liabilities.

Adherence to the basic rules of netiquette can alleviate problems and help cast your employees and your organization in a favorable light.

Netiquette Guidelines for Employees

1. **Beware of hidden readers.** If confidentiality is an issue, don't use unsecured e-mail. You may intend to send an e-mail to one person. But an inaccurate keystroke or the recipient's decision to forward your message could land your e-mail on dozens, hundreds, or thousands of unintended readers' screens. Never use e-mail, without adequate precautions, to communicate trade secrets, proprietary information, or any news that could damage the organization or its employees were the message to be read by an unintended reader.

2. **Write as though Mom were reading.** Regardless of the intended reader, write your message as though your boss, the media, or Mom were reading. People treat e-mail too casually, sending electronic messages they would never say aloud or record on paper.

3. **Remain gender neutral.** You never know where your e-mail will land, so avoid sexist language that could offend or irritate others. Your intended reader may be a male, but the ultimate decision-maker could be the female executive (the hidden reader) who receives a forwarded copy of your orig-

inal message. Send a message full of masculine pronouns
(he, his, him, etc.), and you may turn someone off and lose
this business relationship for good.

4. **Keep the organization's harassment and discrimination
   policies in mind.** Eleven percent of U.S. employers with
   written policies in place have defended sexual/racial harass-
   ment/discrimination claims based on employee use of e-mail
   and the Internet.[2] All electronic communication should adhere to the rules set forth in the organization's harassment,
   discrimination, and information management policies.

5. **Don't use e-mail to let off steam.** Upset or angry? Compose
   yourself before typing your message. Once you hit "send,"
   your e-mail is on its way through cyberspace and probably
   can't be retrieved. Don't take the chance of sending a
   poorly worded or inflammatory message that could worsen
   an already difficult situation or trigger litigation. Even if
   communication is urgently needed, ask a trusted colleague
   to read your document before you send it. If you have the
   luxury of time, give yourself up to forty-eight hours to calm
   down before sending a potentially damaging message.

6. **Control the urge to "flame."** More biting than a thoughtlessly worded message, an e-mail flame is a document that
   is hostile, blunt, rude, insensitive, or obscene. Flames are
   unique to e-mail, as the slow pace of snail mail does not
   accommodate immediate, heated reactions. Flames, and the
   obscene and abusive language that feeds them, have no
   place in a business environment.

7. **Respect others' time.** E-mailboxes stuffed with recipes,
   jokes, advertisements, and requests for charitable dona-
   tions can drain productivity and waste bandwidth. Do not
   use the company computer system to send, forward, or
   reply to spam (electronic junk mail).

8. **Never reply to spam.** If you are on the receiving end of a
   spam mailing, do not reply to the "unsubscribe" option.
   Often, your reply accomplishes just the opposite, confirming your e-mail address and encouraging the sender to for-

ward or sell it to other spammers. Replying to spam also
can be a waste of time, as senders sometimes use one-time-
only addresses to blast the spam into cyberspace. Your irate
reply could land in a black hole. So why bother? For more
on spam, see Part 5.

9. **Do not mail to the world.** Send e-mail messages only to
   readers with a legitimate need for your information. Mail
   to your group list only when it is appropriate for everyone
   on the list to receive the message. Do not reply to a message
   unless you have something to contribute.

10. **Copy with care.** Sending a carbon copy (Cc) or blind car-
    bon copy (Bcc) to a recipient who doesn't need to read your
    message wastes everyone's time. As a rule, address your
    message to the person you want to motivate to act and send
    carbon copies strictly as a courtesy. Carbon copy recipients
    are not required to reply to messages. So don't get upset
    when a response is not forthcoming.

11. **Don't oversell your message.** Just because you have the
    ability to mark messages "urgent" doesn't mean you
    should. Reserve the "urgent" classification for messages
    that demand immediate action.

12. **Ask permission to forward material.** Do you subscribe to
    an e-zine or electronic newsletter that might be of interest
    to an associate or customer? Don't hit "forward" without
    asking permission of the individual who originally sent the
    material as well as your intended recipient. Forwarding
    copyright-protected material without permission could
    land you and your employer in hot water.

13. **Inquire about attachments.** All employers should address
    attachments in their written e-mail policies. Some organiza-
    tions go so far as to prohibit the opening of e-mail attach-
    ments altogether. Before sending an attachment, ask if the
    reader would prefer to receive the information as an attach-
    ment, in the field as part of the message itself, or via fax,
    snail mail, or messenger service.

14. **Incorporate a salutation and signature.** As mentioned
    above, e-mail is a contextual medium. Your salutation and

signature establish your role in the document's history, no matter how often it's forwarded. As an added benefit, your signature signals the end, sparing your reader the aggravation of scrolling the screen for more copy.

15. **Beware the exclamation point!!!** Some writers try to enliven their e-mail and generate reader interest by slapping an exclamation point onto the end of nearly every sentence. Don't fall into this trap!!! Pump up your writing with descriptive factual language and well-crafted sentences, instead.

16. **Resist the urge to capitalize.** Eager for reader attention, many e-mail writers use all capital letters. Bad idea on two counts. For one thing, the eye is accustomed to reading a mix of capital and lowercase letters. Writing uppercase-only messages will slow the reader down and may impede understanding and acceptance of your message.

    Another concern is that readers sometimes interpret messages written in capital letters as the electronic equivalent of shouting. Write entirely in uppercase, and you run the risk of offending and losing recipients before they ever start reading. Another concern: Were your message to be entered into evidence during litigation, your opponent or the jury might draw conclusions about your attitude or state of mind based on your "shouting."

    Do yourself and your readers a favor. Stick with standard sentence style.

17. **Apply the same rule to lowercase letters.** Think an e-mail message that's written entirely in lowercase letters conveys a breezy, informal tone? Think again. Business correspondence that is written entirely in lowercase is likely to paint a picture of you as a lazy, unprofessional writer.

18. **Keep an eye on spelling, grammar, and punctuation.** Your readers will. You wouldn't walk into the president's office or a customer's showroom and start speaking gibberish. Why would you send an e-mail message that is a written form of gibberish? Professionalism extends to all forms of communication: written, verbal, and electronic.

19. **Think before requesting a receipt.** Imagine writing a crucial
    e-mail message that must be read and acted on. Short of
    receiving an electronic response, how can you be certain
    your message has been received and read?

    The quickest, easiest route to peace of mind is to select
    the "receipt notification" option on your screen. When the
    reader opens your message, you will be notified automati-
    cally. It is, however, a good idea to exercise caution with
    this option. Some readers may resent the implication that
    you do not trust them to open and read their e-mail.

    A bigger problem: If you send a message—complete
    with a request for an electronic receipt—to thousands (or
    tens of thousands) of coworkers, the resulting traffic might
    cause the e-mail system to shut down and business to be
    interrupted. To prevent this type of disaster, employers
    should outlaw the unauthorized distribution of e-mail mes-
    sages to the entire workforce.

    In a pressing situation, the better option might be to
    phone your recipient with a quick heads up that the mes-
    sage is on its way, and that you would appreciate a timely
    response.

20. **Keep your editorial comments to yourself.** What to do if
    you receive an e-mail message that is short on style but long
    on mechanical and grammatical errors? Keep your editorial
    comments to yourself. Just as few speakers appreciate hav-
    ing their grammar corrected publicly by coworkers, there
    are not many e-mail writers who would enjoy receiving an
    unsolicited critique of their electronic writing. Leave that
    job to management or the professional writing coach your
    employer brings on board to help employees polish their
    electronic writing skills.

21. **Treat others as you would have them treat you.** If you re-
    ceive someone else's e-mail by mistake, don't trash it. Hit
    "reply" to redirect it to the sender, along with a brief note
    about the mix-up.

    Many companies automatically affix a warning to
    e-mail messages, advising errant recipients how to handle
    e-mail they mistakenly receive. When transmitting e-mail
    subject to the attorney-client privilege, lawyers typically

affix a privilege legend to minimize the likelihood that the attorney-client privilege will be violated if a third party gets a misdirected e-mail. Avoid undermining the privilege legend's utility; do this by addressing it within your written e-mail policy and netiquette guidelines and instructing employees on its proper use. Employees need to use the privilege legend only when appropriate; overuse can undermine its effectiveness.

22. **Consider e-mail's limitations.** E-mail may be the best way to deliver news fast, but it's not necessarily the best route to a quick reply. Your reader is under no obligation to check incoming messages regularly, if at all. It may be inappropriate to send a follow-up message demanding to know why a recipient has not responded to your message.

    For an immediate response to a pressing issue, don't rely on e-mail. Instead, pick up the phone or schedule a face-to-face meeting.

23. Write a descriptive subject line that tells readers what your e-mail is about. Don't let a vague, misleading, or nondescript subject line stop recipients from opening, reading, and acting upon your message.

Recap and E-Action Plan

E-Mail Rule #7: Establish and Enforce Rules of Online Etiquette

1. Use your e-mail policy to enforce online etiquette, or netiquette, rules.

2. Adherence to netiquette guidelines keeps employees' content clean and employers' liabilities in check.

CHAPTER 8

Special Netiquette Considerations for Managers

E-Mail Rule #8: Apply E-Mail Rules Consistently—from Summer Interns to the CEO

Executives and managers should, of course, adhere to the basic rules of netiquette as outlined in the previous chapter. In addition, there are a handful of special netiquette considerations that apply solely to those who supervise employees. Consider the following guidelines when developing your netiquette policy for managers.[1]

1. U.S.-based managers should regularly remind employees that the organization has the right to monitor employee e-mail. Don't allow employees to assume they have an expectation of privacy when it comes to the organization's computer assets.

2. Enforce the organization's e-mail policy consistently. More than 50 percent of employers report terminating or otherwise disciplining employees for violating company e-mail policy.[2] Spell out rules, violations, and penalties clearly in your written e-mail policy. Be fair and consistent with en-

forcement. Do not allow one employee or group of employees any special consideration or second chances other employees do not enjoy equally.

3. Be realistic about the organization's personal-use policy. Thirty-nine percent of employers allow employees free and unrestricted personal use of office e-mail, while 24 percent ban all personal use.[3] While workplace e-mail is intended primarily as a business tool, e-mail may be the only way for some employees to keep in touch with family and domestic partners during working hours. On the other hand, total prohibitions on nonbusiness use may be easier for employees to "interpret." Determine your approach and spell it out clearly, along with penalties for violations, in your written e-mail policy.

4. Never use e-mail to fire employees or deliver bad news. Lacking the benefit of body language, facial expression, and intonation, e-mail is the worst way to deliver bad news to employees. Whether your objective is to terminate an employee or notify a department head of budgetary cutbacks, demonstrate respect for your employees by delivering bad news in person. A one-on-one meeting will give the employee the opportunity to ask questions and absorb the shock of bad news. And, should a wrongful termination lawsuit follow, personal notification may cast management in a better light than electronic notification would.

Real-Life E-Disaster Story: The CEO's Devastating E-Mail

When the CEO of Cerner Corporation opted to use e-mail to express his displeasure over employee performance, he hoped to motivate his 400 managers to act. They acted all right, posting the CEO's angry message on Yahoo!®, where it was read by a hidden audience of 3,100 Cerner employees, as well as financial analysts, investors, and Yahoo! subscribers. The result: Cerner's stock valuation, which was $1.5 billion the day the CEO's e-mail was sent, plummeted 22 percent, from $44 to $34 per share, in just three days. An excerpt from the CEO's devastating e-mail follows:

"We are getting less than 40 hours of work from a large number of our K.C.-based EMPLOYEES. The parking lot is sparsely used at 8 a.m.; likewise at 5 p.m. As managers—you either do not know what your EMPLOYEES are doing, or you do not CARE. You have created expectations on the work effort which allowed this to happen inside Cerner, creating a very unhealthy environment. In either case, you have a problem and you will fix it or I will replace you.

NEVER in my career have I allowed a team which worked for me to think they had a 40-hour job. I have allowed YOU to create a culture which is permitting this. NO LONGER . . .

You have two weeks. Tick, tock."[4]

5. Do not use e-mail to discuss an employee's performance with other managers. You are not required to like every employee personally, but you are obligated to treat each worker with professional courtesy. If you need to discuss an employee's professional shortcomings with the human resources director or instruct a department head to terminate an employee who just isn't working out, do so in person and behind closed doors.

E-mail is fraught with too many dangers for sensitive or confidential communication. You could strike your group list key accidentally, sending negative comments about an employee's work to everyone in the organization. You could type in the address of the employee in question, rather than that of the human resources director, and alert the employee (and the employee's lawyer) to your feelings and comments.

Worst-case scenario: If the employee in question were to file a workplace lawsuit, alleging a hostile work environment or wrongful termination, your electronic discussion with the human resources director could come back to haunt the organization. Remember, e-mail messages, like written performance reviews and other documents, may be subject to discovery and subpoena in litigation. In the event of trial, your e-mail messages concerning this employee could be used as evidence against the organization.

Unless you are willing to risk a breach of security and have your words read by an unintended reader, do not use e-mail. It simply is not secure enough.

6. Do not rely on e-mail to the exclusion of personal contact. To varying degrees, your employees, customers, and suppliers all crave human interaction. While some people may be content to communicate electronically nearly 100 percent of the time, others may feel slighted or unappreciated unless you maintain ongoing personal contact. Even in the age of e-mail, relationship skills remain at the heart of long-term business success. Supplement your e-mail communication by holding regular meetings with your staff, customers, and important suppliers.

7. E-mail is a contextual medium. Do not use e-mail if there is any chance your message will be taken out of context or misunderstood. If your message is complex, technical, or otherwise in any danger of being misinterpreted, opt for a telephone call or a personal meeting instead of e-mail.

If your message is a reply, be sure to include the original message with your response to keep the contextual string intact.

8. Do not rely solely on e-mail to communicate e-mail policies to employees. Create a sense of policy ownership among employees by holding e-mail policy training sessions. Outline e-risks and explain why the organization has established rules and policies. See Part 7 for comprehensive training tips.

Recap and E-Action Plan

E-Mail Rule #8: Apply E-Mail Rules Consistently—from Summer Interns to the CEO

1. Executives and managers can, and routinely do, write e-mail messages that result in electronic disaster. Don't assume the people who sit in corner offices know what constitutes appropriate online content and conduct. Establish and enforce netiquette guidelines with executives, officers, managers, and supervisors in mind.

CHAPTER 9

LISTSERV® Policy
E-Mail Rule #9: Impose Policies and Procedures to Control LISTSERV Participation and Content

LISTSERV is software that allows users to employ e-mail for online discussion. LISTSERVs typically are open to members who subscribe via e-mail. Once they have subscribed, users receive all e-mail that's sent to the LISTSERV address.

LISTSERVs are commonly used for group communication among remote parties with similar business or personal interests. When used properly, LISTSERVs can be a great source of industry information and interaction. But as any subscriber knows, when used improperly, they also can waste time, cause embarrassment, and trigger the occasional disaster.

LISTSERV Dangers

Using a LISTSERV is as easy as sending or receiving any e-mail message. The system's ease, however, can be its greatest challenge. If you take advantage of your system's "autocomplete" feature or accidentally click "reply all," private messages may inadvertently land on the screens of thousands of industry colleagues.

Another problem: Messages sent to LISTSERVs typically

49

are archived for future reference. LISTSERV archives often are published on the Web and referenced by a search engine. Therefore, it is almost impossible to stop readers from finding and reading online LISTSERV postings and "admissions." Subscribers' embarrassing, angry, or otherwise inappropriate comments live forever.

Take Stock of Employees' Online Group Discussion Subscriptions

Scenario: During lunch breaks, Gina routinely used the office computer system to check her stock portfolio and make trades. One day, Gina decided to throw caution to the winds and short sell a medical device manufacturer's stock, hoping the stock price would drop quickly, boosting Gina's bottom line. Unfortunately, shortly after Gina's transaction, rumors of pending Food and Drug Administration (FDA) approval of the manufacturer's newest product hit the market. In two short hours, the stock price rose $6 per share, dashing Gina's hopes for her portfolio.

Desperate, Gina took the market into her own hands. Using her employer's e-mail system, she sent an "anonymous" (and as it turned out devastating) posting to a stock bulletin board. Posing as a company insider, Gina claimed the FDA's pending announcement would be nothing more than a "no action" letter requesting further information from the manufacturer.

As Gina's rumor took hold, nervous investors started unloading the stock. By the end of the most hectic trading day in the company's history, the stock was down $12 a share, reducing the company's market capitalization by nearly $100 million.

Determined to unearth the rumor's source, the manufacturer tracked Gina's "anonymous" e-mail message not only to her employer, but to the computer workstation on her desk. The manufacturer vowed to pursue Gina for triggering a devastating decline in the company's stock price. In addition, the manufacturer announced plans to pursue Gina's employer for failing to manage her online activity.

Because employers can be held responsible for employees' wrongs, Gina's employer found itself defending both its actions and its corporate pocketbook.

Implement Policy to Control LISTSERV Participation and Content

Just how popular is LISTSERV for business and personal e-communications? Extremely.[1]

■ Number of public lists   72,830

■ Number of local lists   189,340

■ Total number of lists   262,170

■ Total membership (public and local)   155,205,556

■ Total messages delivered on one
  representative day   32,963,938

If organizations allow employees to participate in LIST-SERVs or similar online discussion groups, rules should be established and enforced. This includes the implementation of policy that clearly spells out what type of LISTSERVs employees may subscribe to, whose authorization is needed to participate, and what employee-subscribers may, and may not, say.

Employees who are authorized to participate in work-related LISTSERVs should be required to affix a content statement to all correspondence. Drafted by the organization's lawyer with input from the e-risk management team, the organization's LISTSERV content statement should inform outside LISTSERV participants that the subscriber's comments are personal views, not those of the organization.

Recap and E-Action Plan

E-Mail Rule #9: Impose Policies and Procedures to Control LISTSERV Participation and Content

1. A tremendous source of industry information when properly used, LISTSERVs can pose dangers to employers when used improperly by employees.

2. Use written rules, e-mail policy, and procedures to control employees' LISTSERV participation and content.

CHAPTER 10

Corporate Road Warriors

E-Mail Rule #10: Don't Leave Home Without E-Mail Policies and Procedures

When employees treat laptop and handheld computers carelessly, leaving them in hotel rooms, rental cars, and airports, the organization's computer assets and confidential information are up for grabs. A growing problem, laptop theft in the United States accounted for as much as $5 million in losses in 2002, a five-fold increase over the highest losses reported in 1997.[1]

Institute E-Rules for Remote Workers

If your organization employs sales professionals, you're accustomed to their being out in the field with customers. Perhaps you have equipped your outside sales force with handheld computers, so they can write and e-mail orders back to the office at the close of business each day. It's a fast and efficient system that works great, until a handheld is lost or stolen.

Suddenly, you find yourself with no proof or evidence of orders—a big problem if your salespeople have been hoarding orders rather than transmitting them to the office at the end of each working day.[2] It's an even bigger problem if a handheld containing proprietary information has landed in the hands of a competitor with no qualms about data theft.

According to a survey by the International Association of Administrative Professionals (IAAP) and The ePolicy Institute, 66 percent of executives carry wireless handheld devices. Fully 83 percent take their laptops or handhelds on the road when they travel. Another 24 percent report lost or stolen devices.[3]

Real-Life E-Disaster Story: Road Warrior Woes

During the Persian Gulf War, a British military officer left a laptop computer unattended in a locked car. When the car and its contents were stolen, military command assumed the laptop had been hacked and security breached. The officer, whom some would say was guilty of nothing more serious than treating a laptop too casually, was court-martialed as a result.

Marry Policy to Technology

Any organization that uses e-mail for customer transactions must develop rules to ensure that electronic records are properly maintained and readily available to fill orders, address customer questions, or defend legal claims. Why invest in technology to improve your business without investing in policies and practices that maximize effectiveness and minimize risk?

Recap and E-Action Plan

E-Mail Rule #10: Don't Leave Home Without E-Mail Policies and Procedures

1. Develop and implement rules for road warriors before new systems go live and high-tech gadgets leave the building.

2. Establish e-mail rules to ensure that the organization can always locate and access important e-mail.

3. Institute policies requiring salespeople to transmit orders to the organization on a daily basis or other appropriate interval.

4. Educate road warriors about the costs and liabilities of lost and stolen hardware and data. Reinforce the need for employees to keep a sharp eye and firm grip on laptops and handhelds.

5. Consider establishing backup procedures to protect data in the event that transportable computers are lost or stolen.

6. Limit the amount of confidential or proprietary data stored on laptops and handhelds.

7. Take advantage of technological tools, including antitheft software, encryption, and cables/locks that secure laptops to hotel room furniture.

CHAPTER 11

Failure to Establish or Enforce Policy

E-Mail Rule #11: Rules Exist for Businesses That Want to Remain in Business

In the eyes of the law, it's unclear which is worse: having a policy you don't follow, or having no policy at all. Regardless, in the current business environment, neither approach is acceptable. Organizations must not only have e-mail rules; they also must ensure that employees are aware of, understand, and adhere to them.

Vicarious liability (and the related legal concept of *respondeat superior*) is the legal term used when an organization is held responsible for the bad actions of its employees. From a legal perspective, a written policy is one of the most effective tools an organization has to protect itself from vicarious liability claims.

Should the Employer Be Held Responsible? You Be the Judge

Let's say a female employee sues her employer for sexual harassment or related claims. To prove her claim, she offers inappropriate jokes and obscene photos e-mailed to her by a male supervisor. If the organization has an e-mail policy prohibiting sexual content, naked images, harassing conduct, or offensive content, and if the organization conducts mandatory e-mail policy training, should the employer suffer?

If the organization is conscientious enough to have an e-mail policy and train its employees, then perhaps the employer should not be penalized for bad acts that fall outside the offender's job description. In certain circumstances, the law recognizes that an employer who makes reasonable efforts through policy and training to prevent employees from creating a hostile work environment should not necessarily be liable for the bad acts of an individual.

This was confirmed by the Supreme Court of the United States in the seminal cases *Faragher v. City of Boca Raton* and *Burlington Industries, Inc. v. Ellerth*. In both cases, the court made clear that the reasonableness of the employers' conduct— including the establishment of good policies, supported by employee training—may form a defense from liability for sexual harassment or creation of a hostile work environment, triggered by an employee's bad acts.[1]

Establish Rules, Enforce Policy, Avoid Disasters

Scenario: A female employee of a publicly traded company complained to management that her coworkers were violating e-mail policy by accessing and transmitting naked images and engaging in other prohibited conduct. Following the offended employee's complaint that the firm was not enforcing its own policy, management investigated.

The investigation revealed that numerous employees were violating the organization's e-mail policy; those violations carried penalties up to and including termination. Confronted by the reality of a sexual harassment and hostile work environment claim, and its own failure to follow e-mail policy, the firm summarily terminated 50 employee-violators. A tremendous blow to the workforce, the mass firings could have been avoided had the firm adhered to its own policy from the beginning, making an example out of one violator before other employees followed suit.

The Law Appreciates Consistency

Not surprisingly, the inconsistent enforcement of e-mail rules creates headaches for employers. Take the case of the employer whose e-mail policy prohibits sending any message that could be considered "offensive or discriminatory to persons or groups based on nationality, gender, race, sexual orientation, age, etc." As a direct result of that policy, employees have been disciplined on three separate occasions for transmitting inappropriate jokes about Asians, African Americans, and women.

In this case, an in-house accountant has e-mailed the entire accounting department a joke that begins, "Why do so many old people work at the supermarket?" Offended by the joke, a 60-year-old female employee meets with her supervisor to register a complaint and asks that appropriate action be taken. The supervisor's response: "Everybody gets old. That's life."

After six years without advancement, the female employee concludes (based largely on this conversation with her supervisor) that her boss discriminates against seniors. Even without any real evidence of underlying age discrimination, she might be able to successfully advance the argument that the supervisor's failure to punish the offending e-mail user for policy violation is tantamount to age discrimination. Her proof: (1) three offensive e-mail messages that were previously sent; (2) the discipline related to each previous policy violation; (3) the most recent e-mail; and (4) the fact that the supervisor refused to take action and enforce the e-mail policy.

While the supervisor arguably displayed no overt discriminatory behavior, his failure to follow the organization's e-mail policy and punish violators may be sufficient for an age-based class-action lawsuit to take root.

The same principle applies when e-mail rules are enforced among lower-level employees but not among senior management. Many organizations have policies that require all employees to retain and manage e-mail messages but install software that allows the automatic destruction of executive e-mail. Apparently, these organizations fear that executive e-mail could be subpoenaed in the course of lawsuits. What they should fear, instead, is the possibility that a judge will sanction the organization for engaging in a practice that suggests that the executive team has something to hide.

Leave No Room for Interpretation

E-mail policies, like all company guidelines, should be clearly written, easily understood, free of legalese, easily complied with, and consistently interpreted. Not wanting to appear harsh, organizations often are eager to give employees some e-mail latitude, as long as the law is not violated. Instead of clearly stating that company e-mail exists solely for business purposes, these employers use language that is open to individual interpretation. For example, "Personal use of the e-mail system is allowed only to the extent that it does not waste company resources or interfere with the performance of employees' jobs." Seems like a reasonable approach—until you consider the legal implications.

The average employee's interpretation of "waste company resources" probably differs from the interpretation applied by the legal department or the CIO. The significance of interpretation is illustrated by this true story: A few days before Christmas, a collegial employee sent 90,000 coworkers a dancing holiday card, causing several e-mail servers to fail. Faced with a downed e-mail system and unexpected business interruption, management suddenly and clearly recognized why it is risky to allow employees to determine what constitutes system overuse.

Management Loses on Interpretation

Is an employee who wastes hours engaging in personal e-mail each day really in any position to determine if the behavior is "excessive"? Take the case of the employee who regularly devotes two hours a day (a quarter of the work day) to personal e-mail. Fed up, management fires the employee on the grounds that excessive personal use of the system violates e-mail policy.

Filing suit, the terminated employee admits using the e-mail system for nonbusiness purposes, but argues that he was in compliance with the organization's policy and was getting his work done. One legal principle likely to be addressed in this dispute is the fact that ambiguity in language is interpreted against the policy's drafter (the organization). In this case, the organization may lose the argument, all because management wanted employees to relax and have a little fun at work.

Write in Plain English to Limit Risks

When drafting an e-mail policy, instruct your e-risk management team and legal counsel to eliminate any arcane language or legal gobbledygook. The goal is to produce a well-written, clear, and readable e-mail policy. Leave no room for interpretation. Limit questions. Ensure that employees understand what to do—and not to do—via the organization's e-mail system.

Consider, for example, a policy that states, "Employees shall refrain from using or accessing the e-mail system to advance the interests of, or otherwise support, any noncompany-sanctioned philanthropic or charitable activity." In spite of the policy, an employee uses the e-mail system to sell candy to raise money for his daughter's volleyball team. Terminated for violating e-mail policy, the employee claims he read the policy but really had no idea what it meant.

Would twelve reasonable jurors consider the policy "clear on its face," as the organization's lawyer would argue? Doubtful. Thanks to poor writing, the employer could lose this case.

Recap and E-Action Plan

E-Mail Rule #11: Rules Exist for Businesses That Want to Remain in Business

1. Written e-mail policy helps protect employers from vicarious liability claims.

2. The law appreciates consistent enforcement of policy.

3. Draft clear policies. Leave no room for employee misunderstanding or misinterpretation.

PART THREE

Retaining E-Mail Business Records

CHAPTER 12

Retaining Business Records: The Legal Foundation for E-Mail Management
E-Mail Rule #12: Treat E-Mail as a Business Record

From a legal perspective, the process of formally defining, properly identifying, and effectively retaining business records is one of the most important e-mail management activities you can undertake. Your ability to separate business records, both electronic and paper, from nonessential and useless information can have an enormous impact on your organization's business, assets, reputation, and future, should you one day find yourself battling a workplace lawsuit or simply responding to an inquiry from a customer.

What Is a Business Record?

A business record provides evidence for the company of its business-related activities, events, and transactions. Business records are retained according to their ongoing business, legal, compliance, operational, and historical value to the company. A business record focuses on content—the value and future use of information—not format or storage mechanism.

Business records can include:

■ Traditional documents: paper forms, letters, memos, proposals, and other information we typically think of as records

■ Electronic business content: e-mail messages, Instant Messages, and server log files

■ Photographs, recordings, and videos

Whether your organization is public or private, for-profit or not-for-profit, business records are critical to day-to-day activities, including:

■ Decision making

■ Financial and business analysis, forecasting, and reporting

■ Customer service

■ Human resources management

■ Compliance with state and federal laws and regulations

■ Protection of the organization's legal interests

Why Manage E-Mail as a Business Record?

Regardless of how they originate or are stored, business records must be identified clearly and managed properly. E-mail is no exception. In 2001, an estimated 1.4 trillion e-mail messages were sent from North American businesses, up from 40 billion in 1995, according to research firm International Data Corp.[1] Given the business community's growing dependence on e-mail, your organization's legal interests increasingly rest on your ability to define, manage, and access e-mail business records.

What Constitutes an E-Mail Business Record?

Not every message that enters or leaves your organization's e-mail system is a business record. E-mail containing information about lunch appointments, work group discussions, and administrative notices are examples of messages that probably do not have to be managed as "official" business records and may be discarded when no longer needed.

Your organization's welfare depends on your ability to distinguish business records from nonessential information. For example, an internal e-mail inviting employees to the annual company picnic has considerably less value than an external e-mail in which a contractor agrees to complete a specific project for an agreed-on fee. While the picnic announcement has little significance after the event, the contractor's message may be needed in the future to hold the contractor to the price quoted or settle disputes over the quality or scope of work performed. Consequently, the contractor's message is a business record and should be treated as such.

When it comes to business records, management faces a twofold challenge: (1) You must establish a clear definition of a business record to protect the business and legal interests of your organization; and (2) you must communicate that definition clearly and consistently to all employees to ensure that the definition is applied properly, e-mail is managed effectively, and your organization's legal interests are served. The result: Valuable information is retained, and useless information that would otherwise overburden your system is purged.

Business Record or Not? You Be the Judge

Scenario: You are the customer service manager for a large automobile manufacturer. One day, your team receives the following e-mail message:

> To: customerservice@companyx.com
> From: frank@brick.space
> Subject: Airbag problem?
>
> hi, this is frank smith here, and i just bought one of your big SUVs off my neighbor . . . got a great price too! I've always wanted one.

anyhoo, the other day i noticed that the airbag warning light
started flicking on and off, then there was a hissing noise from the
passenger dashboard and it smelled pretty bad.
any idea what the problem is? should i take it in or anything?
thanks!
frank@brick.space

You know Frank's vehicle is currently under a recall program, and you have heard rumors of impending class-action
litigation related to deaths allegedly caused by faulty airbags.

Should you manage this e-mail message as a business record? Apply the principle that records are managed based on
content, and the definition of a business record as *evidence of
business-related activities, events, and transactions with ongoing business, legal, compliance, operational, or historical value.*
Then answer these questions:

1. Would you manage this document as a
   business record if it were in a format
   other than e-mail?   __ Yes __ No

2. Would you place this message in a folder
   and hand it over to the records management department had it arrived in letter
   form via snail mail?   __ Yes __ No

3. If you answered yes to question 2, is there
   any reason why the e-mail format should
   change the need to manage the message
   in a formal way?   __ Yes __ No

4. If you answered yes to question 3, please explain your
   reasoning. _____

5. Does the message provide evidence of
   business activities, events, or transactions, or does it have ongoing business,
   legal, or operational value?   __ Yes __ No

What Your Answers Mean

If you answered yes to questions 1, 2, and 5, congratulations.
This e-mail clearly is a business record. It is a written communi-

cation from someone who owns and is experiencing problems with your product, and it must be managed with appropriate care.

The operational value of the e-mail could come from a number of sources, including warranty service, customer satisfaction, compliance value, or legal value, as detailed below.

Warranty Service Value

Although Frank is not the original owner, the vehicle may still be under a transferable warranty. If so, the new owner needs to know how to receive warranty service or transfer the warranty.

The e-mail may be used to track warranty claims, as it provides valuable anecdotal evidence of the problem.

Customer Satisfaction Value

As an admirer of your product, Frank is likely to return as a customer tomorrow if he is treated well today. Perhaps Frank's e-mail could even be incorporated into a Customer Relationship Management (CRM) or knowledge-base system designed to help other customers with a similar problem.

Compliance Value

The vehicle is under a recall program related to the problem Frank has described. While your company may have an obligation to inform all vehicle owners about the recall, Frank is not the original owner. However, since his e-mail has put the company on notice that he owns a vehicle under recall, you may have an obligation to inform him of the recall.

This e-mail should be managed as a business record on its compliance value alone. In addition, the company should classify any electronic replies to Frank as business records.

Legal Value

You have heard rumors of litigation related to the airbags in Frank's vehicle, and Frank has described what could be a chemical leaking into the vehicle's cabin. This e-mail, therefore, could play a role in potential litigation. Retaining the e-mail along with any records proving you informed the customer of the recall, instructed him to stop driving the vehicle until serviced, and towed his SUV to a garage could help protect you from a future claim filed by Frank.

This is a clear case of one little e-mail packing a potentially powerful punch. The content justifies retaining and managing it as a business record.

How to Determine if E-Mail Is a Business Record

1. You need the e-mail to prove a business-related event or activity did or did not occur.

2. You need the e-mail to demonstrate a transaction: what was purchased or sold, for how much, in what quantity, when it was delivered, or where it went. Even if only some of this information may be gleaned, the e-mail may still be a business record.

3. You need the e-mail to identify who participated in a business activity or had knowledge of an event. All address lines (To, From, Cc, and Bcc) may be equally important.

4. The e-mail has legal or compliance value.

5. You need the e-mail to support facts you claim to be true, since the person with direct knowledge of the facts is not available to testify.

6. The e-mail addresses a public official's activities, an investment broker's client communications, or another topic specifically covered by law or regulation.

Legal Reasons to Manage E-Mail Records

E-mail business records help protect and promote your organization's legal interests when evidence of business activities is needed. E-mail would be an important part of the evidence pool, perhaps the only source of evidence, if your organization were:

1. Battling lawsuits filed by shareholders, customers, competitors, or others.

2. Assisting authorities in the investigation and prosecution of criminal acts committed by employees, customers, partners, etc.

3. Complying with laws governing what your business must do (pay taxes) and must not do (pollute the environment), how it must treat customers, and so on.

4. Adhering to governmental (SEC), self-regulatory (NASD), and industry standard (ISO) regulations and policies.

5. Establishing contractual and other forms of business relationships with suppliers, partners, and customers engaged in buying and selling goods and services.

Recap and E-Action Plan

E-Mail Rule #12: Treat E-Mail as a Business Record

1. Consider how your organization defines business records. If appropriate, develop a new definition and make it part of your policy regime.

2. Update records, policies, and definitions to include e-mail and other electronic formats.

3. Manage information based on its business, legal, compliance, operational, or historical value, rather than the casualness of its creation or its storage medium.

4. Capture and retain complete e-mail records—message content and metadata (data that manages or describes the data).

5. Ensure authenticity by reproducing e-mail messages exactly as they were created.

6. Have ready access to e-mail as needed. Be able to locate it by content.

CHAPTER 13

E-Mail Business Record Retention

E-Mail Rule #13: Retain Business Record E-Mail According to Written and Enforced Retention Rules

A survey by the American Management Association, *US News & World Report,* and The ePolicy Institute reveals that 50 percent of the nation's largest employers have no e-mail retention and deletion policy in place.[1] This is an oversight with profound implications. Because most organizations now rely on e-mail for critical business communication and activities, it stands to reason that at least some e-mail should be classified as a business record and retained and managed according to written rules and policies.

It is, of course, difficult to manage e-mail business records long term without a method for consistently and reliably identifying which messages are business records. Employee training is essential. If employees don't understand which e-mail messages (created and received) should be retained, it's likely important e-mails will be mismanaged, lost, or purged.

What Is Records Retention and Why Apply It to E-Mail?

Records retention is a systematic way of identifying, retaining, managing, and disposing of business records, along with documents and other materials that don't rise to the level of a record. Business records are retained based on their value, rather than their creation, transmission, or storage format. Records retention rules should apply equally to paper and electronic information, as courts, regulators, investigators, and auditors generally don't view electronic information any differently from paper for purposes of retention. E-mail or paper, business records are expected to be managed properly.

While electronic and paper records both require management, the reality and process of retaining e-mail business records differs from paper record retention. E-mail retention poses three main challenges: (1) overwhelming volume; (2) costs related to capturing, indexing, and migrating messaging to fresh storage media, as well as weeding through e-mail to locate specific messages; and (3) unique digital characteristics that impact retention and long-term management.

Records Have a Lifespan

Fundamental to records retention is the fact that records have a lifecycle, complete with a beginning, middle, end, and all the messy in-between stages. Records must be managed according to their value to the organization and for the length of their lifespan, from creation to disposition.

Scenario: Your CEO issues an internal e-mail memo, announcing an upcoming and historic merger. What is the lifespan of that e-mail? Should you identify and retain it as a business record because it contains information necessary to let your business group know of the merger and its impact? In this case, the answer is probably no. The message's initial value was to provide administrative notice to employees. Thus, once you've notified the troops and the merger has occurred, the instructions and the e-mail have negligible ongoing operational value.

On the other hand, were the merger subject to regulator

scrutiny, then all merger-related communications probably should be retained for a time specified by regulation. In this case, the e-mail's lifespan would be longer than required by its administrative value. To ensure proper retention, always incorporate legal and compliance requirements into the retention period.

There's a third way to value this e-mail: The merger may continue to have historical value if it transforms the corporation into a leading multinational public entity, and the CEO is recognized as a revolutionary business leader. Given that scenario, the company archivist could determine that all the CEO's merger-related communications have historical significance and must be retained permanently.

Other Factors Affecting Record Lifespan

If and when a court seeks to determine if the retention period for a given record is reasonable, it will review legal requirements, industry standards, and other practices in which the organization engages. Consistency in developing and implementing retention periods for both paper and electronic records may be viewed as inherently more reasonable than destroying all e-mail after a short period without regard to its value (a potentially risky approach employed by many organizations).

Don't Be Afraid to Put Records to Bed

While it is critical to retain important e-mail messages and other business records, it's equally important to establish procedures for the disposal of records once they reach the end of their lifespan. Eliminating "dead" records in accordance with written policy unburdens the organization's resources and ensures that old information cannot return to harm the organization. Your risk-management job is not complete until dead records are gone.

Strive for Complete, Trustworthy, Accurate Records

Because incomplete or altered records have diminished legal and business value, the goal of any effective e-mail retention program is to maintain complete, trustworthy, and accurate records. In the traditional records management world, this is where the concepts of originals and copies came into play. The goal traditionally was to retain original copies, which were most likely complete and accurate.

In the electronic world, where exact copies are effortlessly produced, there generally is no legal difference between an electronic original and its perfect copy.

Regardless, the focus of retention should be ensuring that e-mail records are authentic, trustworthy, and complete, and have integrity. That means retaining as much information as possible from that original e-mail record. An e-mail printed to paper without its routing information and metadata is simply a piece of paper with words on it.

Trustworthy Records Come from Trustworthy Systems

The system used to manage business records includes people, processes, rules, and technologies, all of which must be managed and controlled to create trustworthiness. That trustworthy records generally do not come from untrustworthy systems is a reality recognized by laws and regulations.

Keys to trustworthiness: (1) written rules and policies that dictate every step of the retention and management process; and (2) evidence that employees are trained and follow the rules. This is why e-mail rules are so important to business. They minimize the likelihood that a court, regulator, or other party will doubt the reliability of your e-mail business records.

Are You Ready to Manage E-Mail Business Records?

1. Does "storage" mean the same thing as
   "retention" to you?   __ Yes __ No

2. Does your organization have a records
   management program?   __ Yes __ No

3. Does your organization manage electronic records according to its records
   management rules?   __ Yes __ No

4. Does your organization apply retention
   periods to e-mail records?   __ Yes __ No

5. Has your organization provided employ-
   ees with training on e-mail retention?   __ Yes __ No

6. Does the technology (IT) department dispose of the contents of the e-mail system
   every 30, 60, or 90 days?   __ Yes __ No

7. Have you ever needed an e-mail but were
   not able to retrieve it as quickly as you
   would have liked?   __ Yes __ No

8. Have you ever needed an e-mail but were
   unable to retrieve it at all?   __ Yes __ No

9. If your organization manages e-mail according to retention rules, is e-mail retention based on the date the message was
   created?   __ Yes __ No

10. Do you ever do any business-related
    work using e-mail?   __ Yes __ No

11. Has your organization ever needed e-
    mail to deal with a lawsuit or audit?   __ Yes __ No

12. Will you be able to access any business-
    related e-mail for as long as you need to? __ Yes __ No

13. Does your organization rely on disaster
    recovery backup tapes for long-term e-
    mail retention or storage?   __ Yes __ No

What Your Responses Mean

To get records retention right, you need to rid yourself of the
notion that storage is the same as retention. E-mail records
should be managed according to their value. If you still think it
is okay to get rid of everything in the e-mail system after a short
period of time, think again. Your e-mail records may one day

be needed to respond to a customer or defend the organization's interest in a lawsuit. You must take e-mail records management seriously if your organization is to survive and thrive.

Recap and E-Action Plan

E-Mail Rule #13: Retain Business Record E-Mail According to Written and Enforced Retention Rules

1. A business record provides evidence of business-related activities, events, and transactions.

2. You must develop a means of consistently and reliably identifying business records.

3. Employees require training to distinguish business records from nonessential e-mail.

4. Disposal or purging is as important as retention. Remember that deletion may not mean it is truly gone.

5. E-mail records (like all records) must be complete, authentic, and trustworthy.

CHAPTER 14

Developing Retention Rules
E-Mail Rule #14: Apply Retention Principles to E-Mail Records

The foundation of a sound records management program, a retention schedule is a detailed document that identifies the different types of information that must be retained and managed as business records. It also stipulates how long a record must be kept and may offer a legal justification for a record's retention.

A typical retention schedule might contain the following:

1. Business function code and name for groups of records (records series). For example, a business function code could be "accounting and finance," or "tax."

2. Records series codes and names combine records related to the same topic or having the same function, so they can be managed as a group. "Accounts Payable and Accounts Receivable" is an example of a records series that could be grouped and managed with "Accounting and Finance" records. (Specific business records that make up a records series would, for example, be "ABC Plumbing Co. Invoice.")

3. The type of media on which an identified records series will be retained.

4. The length of time the official copy of a record will be retained.

5. An indication of whether or not a records series contains vital, historical, or permanent records.

6. The law, regulation, or policy that justifies retaining the record.

7. Additional notes and information to help readers understand the classification categories and records series.

Records Series Lifespan

The lifespan of a records series is determined by business and legal considerations. On the business side, it may be important that your salespeople have the ability to call up an original purchase order three years after a purchase. On the legal side, federal, state, and local laws and regulations often mandate specific retention periods. Other legal considerations, such as the Statutes of Limitations, can help you determine proper retention periods, too.

While laws and regulations may not specifically address e-mail (although they increasingly do), it is in your organization's best interests to ensure that e-mail records are retained for the same length of time as paper records relating to the same topic. For example, if you retain paper purchase orders for three years, then retain e-mail purchase orders for 36 months as well. Consistency is key.

Beware Catch-All Retention Periods

For ease of management, some organizations employ a catch-all strategy that treats e-mail messages as a group and retains the entire group for the same amount of time. A typical policy might read: "All e-mail on the server will be erased after 60 days."

While the desire to streamline e-mail management and eliminate excess messages in a timely fashion is commendable, the catch-all approach ignores individual e-mail content and context, undercutting the recommended value-based approach to records management.

Each E-Mail Message May Be Unique

E-mail is a fairly unstructured form of communication. It's possible for people to write whatever they like, regardless of message type (response to a customer's inquiry, memo to staff, etc.).

Furthermore, the ability to forward and attach information to messages enables e-mail to gather information over time. Consequently, every message contains unique information that may be available nowhere else.

Organizations that assume every entry in a database can be discarded after a year, for example, may encounter trouble with e-mail. Content and messages containing unique business information can be lost easily.

On the other hand, there are certain types of e-mail, such as automatically generated responses that go out when visitors complete Web site forms, that can more easily be managed this way, as the content is fixed and changes only periodically.

Remember, retention is driven by content, not medium.

Recap and E-Action Plan

E-Mail Rule #14: Apply Retention Principles to E-Mail Records

1. Your organization has a need to retain e-mail, just like other business records.

2. Catch-all deletion may have made sense before e-mail was a critical business tool used to execute contracts, hire employees, and interact with customers, partners, and regulators. But it certainly makes less sense today.

3. Treating all e-mail messages as a single group with a single retention period, while applying different retention periods to paper records based on their content, is a fundamentally inconsistent approach that could cause problems if a judge questioned why your organization took time to manage paper records based on content but destroyed e-mail messages with no regard to content.

CHAPTER 15

SEC and NASD Regulations

E-Mail Rule #15: E-Mail Retention Periods May Be Determined by Regulatory Bodies

Within the securities industry, the Securities and Exchange Commission (SEC) and National Association of Securities Dealers (NASD) regulate the retention of business-related e-mail. For example, NASD Conduct Rule 3110, "Books and Records," requires brokerage firms, among others, to retain "books, accounts, records, memoranda, and correspondence in conformity with all applicable laws, rules, regulations, and statements of policy."

Some brokerage firms interpret the SEC language to apply to e-mail and Instant Messages: "originals of all communications received and copies of all communications sent . . . (including interoffice memoranda and communications)" are retained "for a period of not less than three years, the first two years in an accessible place."[1] Other firms adopt different retention periods, based on their interpretation of the regulatory directives and requirements.

Among other requirements designed to promote accuracy, longevity, and easy access to trustworthy electronic records, the SEC provides specific requirements for the media and process used for archiving electronic records generally:

1. Electronic records must be stored on nonrewritable and nonerasable media.

2. The system must "verify automatically the quality and accuracy of the storage media recording process."

3. The organization using electronic records must provide regulators with "facilities for immediate, easy readable projection or production of . . . electronic storage media images and for producing easily readable images."

4. The system must "store separately from the original, a duplicate copy of the record."[2]

Recap and E-Action Plan

E-Mail Rule #15: E-Mail Retention Periods May Be Determined by Regulatory Bodies

1. The SEC takes e-mail retention seriously. Need proof? The commission recently fined several brokerage firms millions of dollars for allegedly failing to retain and/or produce e-mail according to SEC 17a-4.

2. Don't wait for e-disaster to strike. Draft your e-mail rules and policies to adhere to applicable laws and regulations. And educate employees to comply with organizational and regulatory guidelines.

CHAPTER 16

Record Retention Versus Backup Tapes or Stored E-Mail
E-Mail Rule #16: Don't Be Set Up by Backup

Is your organization really retaining e-mail and other electronic records, or are you merely relying on backup systems for retention? If you're simply relying on backup, you're asking for trouble.

Backup systems are not designed for record retention. They exist solely for the mass recovery of critical data in the event of a natural or man-made disaster. Information is stored en masse in a format designed to reduce storage volumes and speed wholesale recovery.

Records management, on the other hand, involves more than storing critical information in a known location. Unlike backup systems, which make no provision for the review of individual e-mail records, records management ensures that you have ready access to any given record, whenever you need it.

The Difference Between Retained Records and Retained Backup Tapes

Organizations commonly and mistakenly assume they are engaged in records management when in fact they simply are determining retention periods for backup tapes. Based on the assumption that original data exists, backup retention is neither a legal nor a records management issue. It is nothing more than a business and technological concern.

Backup tapes should be kept only as long as they are needed to ensure that operations can be restored in a timely fashion following a disastrous data loss. IT departments usually adhere to a schedule that creates a backup tape on a daily, weekly, monthly, or quarterly basis. Because there is no reason to keep backup longer, tapes are rotated and recycled routinely. Good idea. Holding on to backups would expose your organization to potentially costly unmanaged risk if a court forced you to search, reformat, and hand over this potential goldmine of information in the course of litigation.

Real-Life E-Disaster Story: Backup Can Be Costly

When a pharmaceutical company was sued, the company provided multiple backup tapes containing electronic records. Later, the company found itself fighting another legal claim. While litigation was in process, the company, as part of the normal course of business, disposed of the backup tapes from the first case, which concluded shortly after the second lawsuit commenced. Opposing counsel argued the company was wrong to dispose of the tapes without first examining them to ensure that they did not contain information relevant to the current litigation. The court agreed and severely penalized the pharmaceutical company.[1]

Retention Location

E-mail messages identified and retained as business records should be periodically moved from live or active systems into a designated records management application, server, or network location. The benefits of transferring records include:

1. Giving authorized persons access to records required for operational and legal purposes. This could be as simple as one e-mail needed to help build a customer service database

or as complex as a series of messages a d attachments required for a lawsuit.

2. Ensuring that the organization's retention and management policies are uniformly applied.

3. Bolstering the trustworthiness of e-mail records by taking them out of the control of the individual most likely to alter or destroy them—their creator.

4. Easing e-mail record searches for business or legal (discovery) purposes via centralized storage and management.

5. Enabling administrators to focus on one system from a management and maintenance perspective.

6. Helping to ensure that e-mail records are disposed of in a uniform manner consistent with organizational policies.

Paper or Plastic: Two Approaches to E-Mail Retention

Proper e-mail retention is no easy task, a fact illustrated by the many strategies and software applications available today. At the most basic level, however, all organizations must answer the same question: Are we going to keep e-mail in its original digital form or print messages to paper and delete electronic versions? Before deciding on paper or e-mail, weigh the features and benefits, pros and cons of each approach.

E-Mail Pros

E-mail messages contain a wealth of information you may want or need to retain for business and legal purposes:

1. **Header information:** e-mail addresses, e-mail server names and routing information, dates, and sender and recipient names

2. **Body content:** text, graphics, sound, hypertext, links, markup, and other types of code that depend on related e-mail messages, software, and Web sites for their meaning and function to be clear

3. **Attachments:** any type of digital information imaginable, including documents, video files, music, images, executable code, software applications, driver files, and, of course, viruses and Trojan horses

4. **Signatures:** found in the text or, in the case of a cryptographic digital signature, embedded in or wrapped around the e-mail message

Digital Details

If you opt to manage e-mail digitally in a central location, instruct system administrators and architects to ensure that the following information is retained and available for searching and retrieval:

- Creator identification
- Creation or transmission date and time
- Receipt date and time
- Recipient identification
- Routing information

Benefits of the Digital Approach

- Easy search and retrieval
- Searchable in multiple ways depending upon structure
- Ability to access metadata and audit trails to show the integrity of the record
- Can be structured to capture one of each message, making employees responsible for determining what to retain
- Allows for compliance with record production in litigation
- May be the only retention approach to satisfy certain regulators

Downsides of the Digital Approach

- Per-seat cost may be high
- May need to build or buy technology to manage content (E-mail management software is currently available. E-mail

Xtender from Legato Systems, Inc., provides good records management functionality.)

■ Requires technology management resources at the outset and throughout its use

■ Enhanced searchability for discovery may produce e-mail that creates liability or embarrassment

■ Requires training for technology staff and other employees

Real-Life E-Disaster Story: Paper Versus E-Mail

In a 2002 case, the court was asked to compel the production of e-mail messages from backup tapes, at an estimated cost of $395,944 for eight storage tapes and $9.75 million for all the backup tapes.

Confronted with the possibility and enormous cost of searching huge volumes of e-mail messages, the defendant argued that the company printed out the important e-mail communications, eliminating the need to produce e-mail backup tapes. In rejecting that contention, the court noted, "The defendants did not show any policy that defined what e-mail should be reduced to hard copy because of its importance."[2]

We're left to wonder: Would the court have rejected the opposition's request for e-mail if the defendant had produced a policy instructing employees how, when, where, and why to retain e-mail in paper form?

The Paper Approach

If your organization decides that printing e-mail on paper is the only feasible way to properly retain it, then develop rules that clearly state when e-mail is to be printed, what should be printed, and where and how printed files should be stored. Consider instructing employees to:

1. Print messages with transmission data and routing information. E-mail without this type of metadata has questionable evidentiary value.

2. Store messages with similar records.

3. Properly organize, label, and store e-mail records in a universal file plan or indexing regime.

4. Secure confidential and privileged material.

Benefits of the Paper Approach

■ Easy to implement the program and train employees

■ Eliminates masses of electronically stored e-mail

■ Limited storage costs

■ Taps few human or technology resources

■ Reduces the need to migrate or refresh data

■ Limits stored e-mail's discovery exposure

■ Reduces the need to apply retention to electronic media and e-records

■ Inexpensive to implement

■ Retention rules easily implemented

Downside of the Paper Approach

■ Evidentiary value of e-mail may be limited in paper form

■ Evidentiary value of e-mail printed on paper is marginalized without printed metadata for each e-mail record

■ No electronic searching

■ Requires compliance and involvement from all employees

■ May not be acceptable to regulators or courts

■ Potential for losing embedded information within messages

What's Lost When Originals Are Deleted?

When e-mail is printed to paper with the original deleted, important information can be lost, including:

1. Embedded information and linked documents. Their loss changes the content, context, and overall meaning of the message.

2. Transmission information and other metadata that could be used to audit the course and chain of custody of the e-mail message.

3. Signatures and other information used to demonstrate the message's integrity, particularly digital signatures, which cannot be reduced to paper in any meaningful way.

Legal Considerations

"The Law is clear that data in computerized form is discoverable even if paper 'hard copies' of the information [have] been produced."[3] Clearly, while retaining e-mail in paper form may be an attractive means of retention, there are legal considerations worth noting:

1. E-mail without metadata is weak evidence. After all, anyone can type a message on a piece of paper.

2. E-mail in electronic form may be easier to search in response to discovery or regulators' requests.

3. Courts can compel access to electronic versions of printed e-records, and you may face consequences if the electronic version is not available.

4. Much can be learned from seeing an electronic record in electronic form, without which the evidentiary value may be diminished.

To date, only one case has addressed the acceptability of the print to paper approach to e-mail retention. That case, *Public Citizen v. John Carlin, in his Official Capacity as the Archivist of the United States of America*, involved a federal agency. While the case was overturned on appeal for other reasons, the lower court made clear that it considered e-mail printed to paper an unacceptable method of retention. The case itself may have no legal bearing on your company, but it is worth considering the court's position as you develop policy.[4]

Note also that regulators may take issue with electronic records retained in paper form. For example, in IRS Revenue Procedure 98-25, which deals with automated data processing systems (not e-mail systems), the Internal Revenue Service specifies that certain e-records may be audited in electronic form. Therefore, it is at least worth considering the ramifications, if any, of failing to retain e-mail messages in electronic form.

European Retention Law

In an apparent response to increased terrorism and the use of e-mail communications among terrorists, the European nations are considering a law to require providers of communications services like e-mail, phone, and fax to retain records for one year. What impact that ruling will have on U.S. businesses is unclear, but ISPs conducting business in Europe may be faced with major new storage headaches.

Recap and E-Action Plan

E-Mail Rule #16: Don't Be Set Up by Backup

1. Don't confuse backup system retention with business record retention.

2. Holding on to backups longer than necessary potentially creates liability concerns.

3. E-mail business records should periodically be moved from live systems to a records management application.

4. Carefully weigh the pros and cons, business and legal, of digital retention versus paper retention.

CHAPTER 17

Software Solutions
E-Mail Rule #17: E-Mail Rules Apply to Automation, Too

Many employers opt for an e-mail records retention program requiring employee involvement. Other organizations, however, rely on software to read e-mail messages and automatically assign them to an existing category or records series in the retention schedule, or to develop self-defined categories based on content. This process is generally referred to as automatic classification, categorization, or filtering.

Autoclassification

The last few years have seen an explosion of software tools and applications aimed at helping organizations manage and classify the deluge of e-mail. Some of these tools automatically classify, route, delete, or otherwise act based on e-mail content.

Products range from simple (scanning e-mail subject lines for target words) to complex (employing a form of artificial intelligence to determine the meaning of an e-mail's text).

Less complex tools are useful for filtering inappropriate content, reducing spam, and preventing the spread of viruses, etc. Tools at the higher end of the scale can automatically apply retention rules at the central e-mail server, with little or no reliance on employees at the desktop level.

Here's how autoclassification of text works: E-mail text is processed into a series of words or phrases. Extraneous filler or stop words such as "a" and "the" are eliminated to speed the process. The words and phrases that remain are compared against known words or phrases, and the e-mail message is categorized based on predetermined rules.

Consider this e-mail, for example:

> To: PeterandBenny@FictitiousCompany.com
> From: Katie@FictitiousCustomer.com
> Subject: Information on New Widget?
> Hi, I saw an advertisement for your latest Widget on television, and was wondering if you could e-mail me more information, as I really like the looks of it.
> Thanks
> Katie

Both the sender and recipient could form the basis of classification, as the e-mail sender's address is external, which could indicate a customer or potential customer. The phrases "latest Widget" and "television" could be used to indicate a response to the company's current advertising campaign. A combination of factors could be used to classify this e-mail as a "customer request" record, kicking off a series of sales responses.

The value of autoclassification stems not only from the ability to categorize and manage e-mail according to a retention schedule or other rules, but also from the fact that management occurs centrally, and e-mail records are automatically captured and moved to a designated records management system. Autoclassification systems often are configured to work hand-in-hand with records management or document management applications.

This can help resolve the problem of employees failing to categorize and move e-mail records off their active systems, and it can add to the overall perceived trustworthiness of record e-mail.

Is Autoclassification Right for You?

Autoclassification is not a panacea. It is only as good as the rules and policies that have been developed to control it. There is still work to accomplish, in terms of building a classification system to reflect your business and legal interests. Ensuring that the software is doing a satisfactory and consistent job often requires constant administration and maintenance.

You should also consider what to retain via autoclassification. The system could be used to capture one copy of every e-mail, even if the captured messages do not meet the definition of a business record, or it could capture any other identifiable category you wish to retain. Some software develops self-defining categories based on the content of messages that are not easily classifiable. This, however, can result in a pile of messages that ultimately needs to be reviewed by a human being.

If you opt not to retain one of everything, you empower the software to dispose of e-mail that (in the software's opinion) meets your description of disposable e-mail. Given the business and legal issues that can arise from inadvertently or purposefully destroying necessary e-mail, this approach would require confidence in the system. It's important to note that autoclassification will likely make mistakes, regardless of configuration.

These systems also can be configured to use a hybrid of automatic and human classification. The system makes preliminary classification decisions, which are confirmed or changed by a member of the staff. This approach can result in a high degree of accuracy. Some systems can even learn this way, being taught where they are making classification mistakes.

Other Software Functions

There are many other software applications available to assist your organization in managing e-mail. Some of the functionality available with software includes:

- Develop and enforce e-mail policies

- Archive e-mail messages

- Retain messages according to defined retention rules

- Develop and apply retention periods, and enable easy disposition

- Allow for easy search and retrieval, through full text searching and other techniques

■ Provide auditing mechanisms to track access and changes to stored messages

■ Conduct monitoring and reporting

■ Access controls for providing authorized parties access to the whole or parts of the system for administration, searching, and conducting of discovery and audits

Benefits of E-Mail Management Software

■ Moves messages off servers and active e-mail systems to increase functionality and speed

■ Allows users ready access to needed messages

■ Allows users to make record-keeping decisions based on content

■ Facilitates records policies and retention rules

■ Protects company business and legal interests by retaining only what is needed

■ Allows users to classify and code individual messages

■ Allows messages to be retained for a requisite period of time

■ Protects confidential and privileged information

Recap and E-Action Plan

E-Mail Rule #17: E-Mail Rules Apply to Automation, Too

1. Software exists to automatically classify, route, delete, or otherwise act on e-mail content.

2. High-end software will automatically apply your retention schedule at the central server, with little (or no) employee involvement.

3. Autoclassification is only as good as the rules and policies that tell it what to do, and it will likely never be 100 percent.

CHAPTER 18

Outsourcing E-Mail Storage and Retention

E-Mail Rule #18: Assess the Legal and Business Ramifications Before Moving E-Mail Off Site

In addition to enterprise-focused tools for managing e-mail, recent years have brought about third-party, or outsourced, e-mail management and storage services. These popular Application Service Providers (ASPs) and Storage Service Providers (SSPs) deliver storage and management services minus the large outlay of capital required to buy or build similar solutions in-house.

What Is an ASP?

Application Service Provider is a new name for an old concept: outsourcing. The contemporary twist: The speed and availability of global network connectivity via the Internet enables sophisticated applications and features to reside in one central location (the ASP) and be delivered to your company over the Internet and accessed through a Web browser.

Storage Service Providers (SSPs) are ASPs that offer remote storage and data management. Quickly becoming the biggest expense in large employers' IT budgets, data storage gobbles up as much as 30 percent of capital expenditures. Outsourcing data storage may cut 10 to 30 percent of your IT budget.[1]

ASP Advantages and Disadvantages

Cost makes the ASP model appealing. Using an ASP is like leasing office equipment rather than buying it outright. You pay a monthly ASP fee, freeing capital that otherwise would be tied up in licensed software.

Service is another ASP advantage. The ASP provides up-to-date software, technical support, maintenance, and other administrative tasks that can be the most expensive part of owning and operating licensed software.

The downside to ASPs also revolves around cost and service. Over the long term, your subscription fee could dwarf a one-time software purchase. Network interruptions, security breaches, and administrative errors result in downtime, which you would not experience (in the same way) were software kept in-house.

Legal Concerns

There is cause for concern when applications or information residing at the ASP data center have business and legal significance, particularly in relation to e-mail context. With data stored off-site, issues of record control may be a problem, particularly for regulators. Regulators and the courts expect the timely delivery of e-mail records. Response time could be hampered by poor service or system outages on the ASP's end. In that regard, care should be taken when selecting an ASP. Select a provider that's likely to be in business over the long haul. Given the stringent e-mail retention requirements imposed by the SEC, brokerage firms and others are increasingly utilizing the services of e-mail outsourcers like Iron Mountain Digital Archives and others for e-mail retention and management.

Outsourcing Rules

One of the keys to a successful relationship with a third-party e-mail management and storage provider is a Service Level

Agreement (SLA) that protects your organization's interests. An effective SLA should address these issues:

1. **System uptime.** For critical systems such as e-mail, expect minimal unscheduled downtime. Be sure your SLA guarantees system uptime and provides fee reimbursements and other remedies when downtime occurs.

2. **Security.** You want a complete list of software, hardware, and practices used to ensure physical, network, and content security. The level of security offered needs to be at least as good as the security you could cost-effectively implement on your own. Security is particularly important when valuable information is moving around the country or the globe. Look for encryption, Virtual Private Networks, and private leased lines, among other features.

3. **Redundancy.** Look for a provider who can quickly respond to a data center disaster with a duplicate set of hardware, software, and Internet access points. If you are using a provider to store critical data, be sure precautions are taken to prevent data from being lost or damaged. Critical data should be backed up and moved off site to another secure facility.

4. **Throughput/capacity.** Because e-mail storage volumes can be large and unpredictable, it's in your best interests to negotiate guarantees regarding the amount of network bandwidth required to store and retrieve data and the costs associated with your storage volume requirements.

5. **Access.** Business, compliance, and legal needs often mandate fast access to stored data. Ensure that data is easily and quickly accessible from your ASP or SSP. To increase the efficiency of their operations, ASPs often will move full storage devices offline as soon as possible—a strategy that may not serve your interests if an offline tape or optical disk needs to be located in a warehouse across the country and loaded into an active device to be searched.

6. **Business continuance.** Avoid ASPs/SSPs that don't have a written plan to transfer data assets to you or a related ser-

vice in the event the ASP/SSP goes out of business or is purchased. Also make sure the ASP will be able to assist you if you need to produce e-mail for litigation. Agree on the fees associated with "litigation support" services before signing the contract. Ensure that technical specifications for hardware and software are available and agreed on. Your organization must be able to access and read data returned by the ASP.

Outsourced Services Available

■ **Internet access and e-mail.** Just as home users pay monthly fees to Internet Service Providers (ISPs), many small and mid-size companies outsource Internet access and e-mail functions.

■ **Server space.** Small and mid-size organizations often rent servers or space on servers from third-party data centers, which offer fast Internet connections and management services that could not be provided in-house for the same cost.

■ **Complete e-mail system.** Billing on a per-user or per-mailbox basis, the ASP operates required e-mail server hardware and software, security systems, and other features configured to the client's needs. The client's own IT administrators access administrative controls over the Internet, allowing them to add and remove users and perform other tasks.

■ **Archiving.** E-mail messages the client company wants to retain are sent over a network to the service provider, which receives and files e-mail according to the client's criteria. Using a Web browser, the client can access, search, and dispose of the retained e-mail over the network.

■ **Physical storage.** Storage drives, tapes, and other devices are moved off site to a storage provider that offers an environmentally controlled and secure facility designed to promote media longevity.

Employee Storage Volumes Create a Slippery Slope

Scenario: Wishing to reduce the overall volume of stored e-mail, an organization enacts a policy that limits the amount of server storage space granted each employee for e-mail. In spite of the written policy, however, management allows certain employees extra storage space. Management also knows some employees are sidestepping policy by moving e-mail to their desktop hard drives and other storage locations.

The problem: Policy is effective only when it is consistently enforced. Allowing employees to maintain personal e-mail treasure troves can lead to big problems should a lawsuit be filed and e-mail required.

The solution: Management sees its biggest problem as employee mailbox size, but it is being short-sighted. The organization should consider a broad range of e-mail management goals:

- Maximizing system performance

- Enabling employees to perform their jobs

- Ensuring ready access to needed messages for as long as required

- Eliminating junk e-mail and nonrecords

Recap and E-Action Plan

E-Mail Rule #18: Assess the Legal and Business Ramifications Before Moving E-Mail Off Site

1. Third-party ASPs and SSPs provide outsourced e-mail storage and management services at a fraction of the initial cost of in-house solutions.

2. Cost and service are ASP advantages—and disadvantages.

3. If third-party services are used, be sure you have access to e-mail records when you need them.

4. Protect your organization's interests with a comprehensive Service Level Agreement.

CHAPTER 19

Educating Employees About E-Mail Retention
E-Mail Rule #19: Make E-Mail Retention Simple for Employees

Obviously, it's difficult to manage e-mail business records long term without a method for consistently and reliably identifying electronic business records. Employee training is key. Unless employees clearly understand which e-mail messages (created and received) should be retained, important e-mails are likely to be inaccessible or disappear.

Because retention schedules generally are large and cumbersome, with up to hundreds of different categories, employees find marking or coding e-mail for retention purposes challenging.

The solution: Seek input from the in-house legal team, records management, IT, HR, and other members of your e-risk management team. Ask how retention and retention coding decisions could be simplified to ensure employee understanding and compliance. A few tips:

1. Assign your team the responsibility of developing a workable process.

2. Get employees involved in the process, as employees are best situated to determine if a particular e-mail is a record.

3. Develop simple coding lists for employees. Coding may be different for different business units. It's unlikely, for example, that the sales and marketing team would have any IRS filing records. Coding e-mail messages according to a classification scheme not only is useful for ensuring that e-mail records are retained for a correct period of time, but also can help protect confidential or privileged information.

4. Make sure proper coding will take employees only a few seconds to make the right selection. Using more time to search for the right code will frustrate employees and may decrease coding accuracy.

5. If employees have difficulty finding the right code, it's likely that e-mail will be put in a catch-all bucket, which defeats coding.

Must We Keep Every E-Mail Forever?

No. Use carefully drafted retention rules to separate the wheat from the chaff. Getting rid of all unnecessary messages, nonrecords, and other business content will greatly reduce the amount of e-mail you are managing over the long haul. Doing so frees hardware, network, and human resources, while reducing the risk of inappropriate or irrelevant e-mail messages returning to hurt or embarrass your organization. Formal retention rules also can help protect you against legal claims stemming from the indiscriminate destruction of e-mail business records, specifically, those you suspect could be requested in the context of future litigation.

The courts agree that not everything a company generates needs to be retained. As one court noted, "We see no evidence of fraud or bad faith in a corporation destroying records it is no longer required by law to keep and which are destroyed in accord with its regular practices. As we have previously observed, storage of records for big or small businesses is a costly item and destruction of records no longer required is not in and of itself evidence of spoliation."[1]

But We Want to Keep Everything Forever

Does your organization retain all your e-mail forever? Congratulations. You're a disaster waiting to happen.

You may not want to focus on classification, copies, drafts, and other retention schedule details. But the fact is that you must.

Don't be misled into believing that the relatively low cost of storage devices and media warrants saving all e-mail forever. It is, in fact, easy to underestimate the amount of "free" disk space required to store the huge volume of e-mail that a 10,000-person organization, for example, would generate over time. In reality, by saving all e-mail forever, you incur numerous costs, including:

- Media

- Hardware

- Software

- Increased time to access

- Migration

- IT time spent managing additional e-mail

- Employee time spent finding needed e-mail

- IT costs related to refreshing or migrating data to new media

- New media costs incurred at the end of the current media's useful life

- Cost of producing e-mail in litigation

- Costs triggered by e-mail's negative impact on litigation

- Costs associated with dormant e-mail risks

As with any business record, your organization needs rules that direct employees on their approach to retaining e-mail. E-mail retention rules at a minimum should include directives to clearly limit retention to what you define as a business record. This is somewhat challenging in the e-mail world, as it means you need to address a variety of issues, such as retention of "nonrecords," drafts, attachments, and duplicates.

Rules for Disposing of E-Mail

Just as you must provide employees with e-mail retention rules, so too must you instruct employees how to effectively and appropriately dispose of e-mail.

1. Instruct employees to dispose of nonrecord e-mail messages immediately after they are no longer needed.

2. Be sure employees consider the organization's retention rules before determining if a message can be disposed of.

3. Never dispose of, alter, or make unavailable any message (including drafts, duplicates, transitory messages, etc.) relevant to an imminent, threatened, or pending lawsuit, investigation, or audit.

4. If you think your organization is about to be sued, do not rush to destroy any related e-mail, including nonrecords and drafts.

5. Protect your employees and organization by insisting that e-mail records disposition adhere to a written policy or retention schedule.

6. If e-mail content is confidential, privileged, or otherwise needs to be kept from others, make sure it is permanently and securely purged from all the media on which it is stored.

7. Eliminate all paper and electronic copies when the retention period is complete.

Training Employees to Spot Nonrecords

It is essential that your employees clearly understand your definition of a business record. Without that awareness, you cannot ensure that the organization's valuable e-mail is being retained and nonrecords are being discarded properly.

To that end, implement an education program that combines written e-mail rules with periodic reminders and training seminars.

An employee, if asked, should be able to determine whether

to retain an e-mail message from a client thanking the employee for an invitation to the organization's annual party. Is this e-mail a record or a nonrecord? Can it be disposed of? A well-trained employee would know this e-mail has little ongoing business value and need not be retained, unless there was a compelling reason to do so.

Without training, employees cannot be expected to know how to assess the value of e-mail. You, the employer, are obligated to teach employees that an e-mail's value is based on content and context—what it says and why it exists.

Rules for Drafts

Unless there are compelling legal or business reasons, there generally is no reason to hold onto the preliminary draft of an e-mail message, provided the final version is properly retained and may be relied on as the official record. The same holds true for e-mail that contains successive drafts of documents.

Retaining multiple drafts and attachments is likely to confuse and complicate matters when you need to find and produce a record. One organization recently learned that lesson the hard way when, in the course of federal litigation, it entered into a battle to determine which version of a contract was the final one. After two weeks of wrangling, the company conceded it was wrong. The court made known its displeasure with the organization for wasting valuable court time attempting to distinguish a draft from the final version of a contract, a dispute that wasn't even germane to the real issues in the case.

Avoid similar disasters by establishing e-mail rules that clearly define final versions versus drafts. Be sure employees know that drafts can be discarded under normal circumstances.

Rules for Duplicates

Duplicates are an unfortunate byproduct of e-mail technology. Every time an e-mail lands on a server or a computer, it makes a copy, propagating the same message multiple times. Unlike the original, these copies deliver little real benefit.

Scenario: An employee drafts an e-mail, complete with attachment, and copies it to all fifty members of a business unit. What should the fifty employees do with their copies?

If you had comprehensive written rules in place, your employees would not have to waste productive time deciding whether to retain or delete electronic copies. Well-trained employees would know that only the "official" copy of the e-mail record, retained by another employee in another location, is needed.

Another way to control the flow of duplicates is to inform employees that only the sender need retain internal e-mail sent to colleagues. If someone other than the sender must take action pursuant to the message, that person also should retain a copy. All other e-mail messages and attachments should be purged from the system when no longer needed.

Instructing employees that recipients are required to dispose of unnecessary duplicates will enhance their comfort level. They will know they are neither violating company policy nor breaking the law when deleting duplicate e-mail.

Don't Leave Employee Compliance to Chance

Teach employees how to deal with unnecessary duplicates from a retention perspective. Instruct the IT staff to configure the system to limit the number of duplicate e-mail messages that are automatically parked on computers. Train employees to send e-mail messages only to those with a need to know. Set rules regarding who is responsible for retention of official e-mail. Explain that printing unnecessary e-mail copies wastes paper and creates one more item that must be searched when the organization is trying to locate needed information.

You may never achieve 100 percent compliance. But you certainly can reduce the number and cost of unnecessary duplicates retained and help your organization get a grip on e-mail overload. All it takes are a few e-mail rules and a comprehensive employee training program.

Manage Multiple Attachment Copies with an Attachment Warehouse

To manage multiple copies of the same attachment, some organizations use an "attachment warehouse," in which only one copy of the attachment is retained. Intended recipients visit the organization's Intranet or other designated location to access and download the attachment.

Recap and E-Action Plan

E-Mail Rule #19: Make E-Mail Retention Simple for Employees

1. Employees determine if an e-mail is a record or nonrecord.

2. Nonrecords stay in their current storage locations.

3. Records are moved to a different physical location for retention.

4. Retention should take place off the active e-mail environment in a place that promotes access, retrieval, and system functionality.

5. Employees code e-mail for retention according to a simplified records retention template.

6. The law department, IT, and records management should work together to make the template user friendly and consistent with current records policies.

7. What remains on the active e-mail system would be transitory or convenience copies of e-mail and nonrecords that the company should not retain, and that could be purged every 30, 60, or 90 days.

   Remember, your organization does not have to keep everything. First, retain e-mail records that are needed, then purge the system of what remains.

8. Technology department issues are addressed by reducing the quantity of stored e-mail. Maximize system performance by removing retained e-mail from the system.

PART FOUR

E-Mail Business Records as Legal Evidence

CHAPTER 20

E-Mail Business Records as Legal Evidence

E-Mail Rule #20: Prepare to Produce E-Mail for Audits, Investigations, or Lawsuits

Our ever-increasing reliance on e-mail for business activities makes it likely your organization will one day need to access and deliver e-mail messages in the course of an audit, investigation, litigation, or other formal proceeding. In fact, computers have become so commonplace that most court battles now involve discovery of computer-stored information.[1]

Business Records Exception to the Hearsay Rule

When hearing evidence in a case, the court normally requires direct testimony from an individual who witnessed, or has first-hand knowledge of, an event. The court normally will not admit hearsay evidence, such as testimony that simply recounts what another person said.

On their own, business records are a form of hearsay. Unless those who created or otherwise knew about a business record during its lifecycle are called to testify, no first-hand testimony about the record would be offered, and it might be excluded as hearsay.

However, recognizing that business records are an important source of evidence, the courts have created an exception to the hearsay prohibition. The Business Records Exception to the Hearsay Rule allows e-mail messages and other business records created and kept in the ordinary course of business to be admitted into court.

This exception addresses the reality that corporations and government agencies typically exist for generations, long past the time the creator of a specific record would be available to testify and be cross-examined about its origins. It also acknowledges that it would be both expensive and difficult for litigants to provide firsthand testimony for every document used in a trial, especially when trials can involve thousands of pages of evidence.

Broad Scope

The courts have required employers to search through and produce huge volumes of e-mail messages in the course of litigation. In one case, an organization was ordered to search 30 million pages of e-mail.

Nearly any e-mail could be required as evidence in court, even those that do not meet the definition of a business record. Seemingly innocuous administrative e-mail notices about a company softball game could be used as evidence if, for example, an employee injured during the game attempted to make a workers' compensation claim.

Laws and Regulations

The legal system today is working to apply existing legal principles and develop new laws to address the business community's widespread reliance on e-mail. That's appropriate, given how prevalent e-mail is within the legal and regulatory worlds themselves. Some jurisdictions allow parties to file court documents via e-mail, while others allow attorneys to communicate with and advise clients via e-mail. Some government agencies allow the submission of official filings via e-mail. They also rely on e-mail to notify the public of government activities.

E-SIGN and UETA

Two of the most important legal e-developments in recent years involve the passage in 2000 of the federal Electronic Signatures in Global and National Commerce Act (E-SIGN),[2] and the 1999 Uniform Electronic Commerce Act (UETA), which most states have now adopted. E-SIGN and UETA, which ensure that e-records, including e-mail records, have the same legal effect as paper records for most purposes in most jurisdictions, remove much of the uncertainty surrounding the use of e-mail for business purposes. They also have spurred regulators and policy makers to draft other laws and regulations establishing requirements and standards for electronic records.

Together, E-SIGN and UETA establish the equivalence between digital and paper-based evidence and signatures on the federal and state levels. Thanks to these two laws, documents and records cannot be discriminated against in legal proceedings merely because they are created in digital form. However, as will be explained in the coming sections, just because e-records are legally acceptable generally does not mean they are sufficient in a particular case.

E-SIGN on Retention of Contracts and Records

If a statute, regulation, or other rule of law requires that a contract or other record relating to a transaction in or affecting interstate or foreign commerce be retained, that requirement is met by retaining an electronic record of the information in the contract or other record that:

(A) accurately reflects the information set forth in the contract or other record; and

(B) remains accessible to all persons who are entitled to access by statute, regulation, or rule of law, for the period required by such statute, regulation, or rule of law, in a form that is capable of being accurately reproduced for later reference, whether by transmission, printing, or otherwise.[3]

UETA on Retention of Electronic Records

(a) If a law requires that a record be retained, the requirement is satisfied by retaining an electronic record of the information in the record which:

(1) accurately reflects the information set forth in the record after it was first generated in its final form as an electronic record or otherwise; and

(2) remains accessible for later reference.[4]

Laws addressing e-mail as a business record come from a variety of other sources, including federal, state, and local statutes and regulations. The policies and practices mandated by industry associations, boards, and standards groups (such as ISO) are another source of regulation that must be considered.

What Makes Good Evidence and Business Records?

Whether business records take paper, electronic, or other tangible form, there are qualities that separate good records—those that can be relied on for business and legal purposes—from bad. The qualities of good business evidence are:

1. **Authenticity.** It is important to be able to demonstrate the origin of a business record, including the identity of the drafter and those who added to or altered it. It also is important to know whether or not an e-mail message is the original or a copy that was altered and forwarded by someone other than the drafter. As detailed in Part 5, security and access controls are valuable for demonstrating the authenticity of an e-mail business record.

2. **Integrity.** A good business record has integrity. Its material content and meaning have not changed since it was originally created. Put controls in place to ensure that business records cannot be altered once they are identified as records.

3. **Accuracy.** While e-mail business records represent facts about business events and transactions, in order to be le-

gally acceptable, an e-mail must be accurate about the facts documented originally, and it must maintain accuracy throughout its life. Failure to show that an e-mail is accurate may limit or prohibit its use for legal purposes.

4. **Completeness.** Unlike paper and other fixed records, there is no inherent quality to ensure that an e-mail record is self-contained and immutable. In fact, e-mail messages are composed of multiple parts—the body, header, attachments, and log files relating to its transmission and receipt—that are all part of a complete record.

   To make it even more challenging, e-mail records often contain links to related documents that are integral to the meaning of the message. For example, a purchase made via e-mail with a link to product specifications that are subject to change without notice can dramatically change the meaning of the e-mail contract or original deal down the road.

5. **Repudiation.** When e-mail is used in the context of business transactions that have contractual significance, there is a risk of repudiation. In other words, a party may refuse to act as promised via e-mail, claiming a different agreement was struck, or, even worse, claiming not to be the individual who entered into the agreement. The greater the value or risk of the transactions, the more significant the consequences of repudiation.

   Protecting against repudiation is a function of good records or evidence. For example, holding someone to a promise or statement depends on your ability to prove that the promise actually was made. That's largely a function of the record's authenticity. Protection against repudiation depends on the trustworthiness of the overall process used to ensure the authenticity, integrity, accuracy, and completeness of e-mail.

Build Evidence Based on Need

In a perfect world, all of your organization's e-mail transmissions would be authentic, accurate, and complete. You could sleep soundly, knowing you were protected against repudiation.

In reality, however, ensuring these qualities requires time, talent, and technology. That investment should be commensurate with the value and potential risk of the transaction.

What Kind of Records Satisfy Regulators?

Generally, regulators are looking for e-records that embody the qualities of good evidence. Some regulators provide guidance to help you architect your e-mail system properly.

Four Steps to Getting E-Mail Records Evidence Right

1. Be sure to involve your lawyers and your tax, audit, and IT staff in the process of walking through the language of relevant rules.

2. Translate legal language into the business and technological reality that reflects your business.

3. Determine how you can build reasonable controls to ensure integrity, accuracy, and completeness for the application.

4. In addition to building a sound system and good evidence, the collaborative process demonstrates the company's eagerness to get it right, a fact that won't be lost on the regulator.

Sample: The Internal Revenue Service

IRS Procedure 97-22 provides guidance to taxpayers who maintain books and records via electronic storage. It offers useful insights into what may be required by regulators.

SECTION 4. ELECTRONIC STORAGE SYSTEM REQUIREMENTS
.01   General Requirements.
(1) An electronic storage system must ensure an accurate and complete transfer of the hard copy or computerized books and records to an electronic storage media. The electronic storage system must also index, store, preserve, retrieve, and reproduce the electronically stored books and records.

(2) An electronic storage system must include:
  (a) reasonable controls to ensure the integrity, accuracy, and reliability of the electronic storage system;
  (b) reasonable controls to prevent and detect the unauthorized creation of, addition to, alteration of, deletion of, or deterioration of electronically stored books and records;
  (c) an inspection and quality assurance program evidenced by regular evaluations of the electronic storage system including periodic checks of electronically stored books and records;
  (d) a retrieval system that includes an indexing system (within the meaning of section 4.02 of this revenue procedure); and
  (e) the ability to reproduce legible and readable hardcopies (within the meaning of section 4.01(3) of this revenue procedure) of electronically stored books and records.

(3) All books and records reproduced by the electronic storage system must exhibit a high degree of legibility and readability when displayed on a video display terminal and when reproduced in hardcopy. The term "legibility" means the observer must be able to identify all letters and numerals positively and quickly to the exclusion of all other letters or numerals. The term "readability" means that the observer must be able to recognize a group of letters or numerals as words or complete numbers. The taxpayer must ensure that the reproduction process maintains the legibility and readability of the electronically stored document.

(4) The information maintained in an electronic storage system must provide support for the taxpayer's books and records (including

books and records in an automated data processing system). For example, the information maintained in an electronic storage system and the taxpayer's books and records must be cross-referenced in a manner that provides an audit trail between the general ledger and the source documents(s).

(5) For each electronic storage system, the taxpayer must maintain, and make available to the Service upon request, complete description of:

    (a) the electronic storage system, including all procedures related to its use; and

    (b) the indexing system (see section 4.02 of this revenue procedure).

(6) At the time of an examination, or for the tests described in section 5 of this revenue procedure, the taxpayer must:

    (a) retrieve and reproduce (including hardcopies if requested) electronically stored books and records; and

    (b) provide the Service with the resources (e.g., appropriate hardware and software, personnel, documentation, etc.) necessary to locate, retrieve, read, and reproduce (including hardcopies) any electronically stored books and records.

(7) An electronic storage system must not be subject, in whole or in part, to any agreement (such as a contract or license) that would limit or restrict the Service's access to and use of the electronic storage system on the taxpayer's premises (or any other place where the electronic storage system is maintained), including personnel, hardware, software, files, indexes, and software documentation.

(8) The taxpayer must retain electronically stored books and records so long as their contents may become material in the admin-

istration of the Internal Revenue laws under § 1.6001-1(e).

(9) The taxpayer may use more than one electronic storage system. In that event, each electronic storage system must meet the requirements of this revenue procedure. Electronically stored books and records that are contained in an electronic storage system with respect to which the taxpayer ceases to maintain the hardware and the software necessary to satisfy the conditions of this revenue procedure will be deemed destroyed by the taxpayer, unless the electronically stored books and records remain available to the Service in conformity with this revenue procedure.

(10) Taxpayers may use reasonable data compression or formatting technologies as part of their electronic storage system so long as the requirements of this revenue procedure are satisfied.

.02 Requirements of an Indexing System.

(1) For purposes of this revenue procedure, an "indexing system" is a system that permits the identification and retrieval for viewing or reproducing of relevant books and records maintained in an electronic storage system. For example, an indexing system might consist of assigning each electronically stored document a unique identification number and maintaining a separate database that contains descriptions of all electronically stored books and records along with their identification numbers. In addition, any system used to maintain, organize, or coordinate multiple electronic storage systems is treated as an indexing system under this revenue procedure. The requirement to maintain an indexing system will be satisfied if the indexing system is functionally comparable to

a reasonable hardcopy filing system. The requirement to maintain an indexing system does not require that a separate electronically stored books and records description database be maintained if comparable results can be achieved without a separate description database.

(2) Reasonable controls must be undertaken to protect the indexing system against the unauthorized creation of, addition to, alteration of, deletion of, or deterioration of any entries.[5]

Recap and E-Action Plan

E-Mail Rule #20: Prepare to Produce E-Mail for Audits, Investigations, or Lawsuits

1. Many court battles today involve discovery of e-mail and other electronic evidence.

2. Nearly any e-mail could be required as evidence in court, even those that fail to meet the definition of a business record.

3. E-SIGN and UETA ensure that e-mail records generally have the same legal effect as paper records.

4. Good business evidence shares the qualities of authenticity, integrity, accuracy, and completeness.

5. Regulators and courts look for e-records that embody the qualities of good evidence.

CHAPTER 21

Records Management
E-Mail Rule #21: Manage E-Mail Business Records to Ensure Accuracy and Trustworthiness

Not all business records are created equal.[1] Courts, regulators, customers, partners, and employees expect records to be complete, accurate, and trustworthy. Ensuring that your e-mail business records serve your business and legal needs requires good management controls and policies.

Legal Versus Reliable

Just because e-mail is generally legal does not necessarily make it trustworthy, complete, and admissible as evidence for litigation. Nor is it necessarily compliant with regulatory requirements. An e-mail business record's admissibility and ability to influence the outcome of a case depend on several factors, with overall integrity topping the list.

While the law is clear on the general acceptability of e-mail business records, it is not specific about how authenticity and trustworthiness should be delivered and demonstrated consistently. Yet to use e-mail as evidence in a dispute, you may need to demonstrate the reliability of your e-mail system and messages.

The way in which an e-mail message is managed, from its creation to the moment it is offered as evidence, is open to attack. Failure to control access to a stored e-mail message may allow someone to suggest that the content was or could have been altered. Failure to retain and provide all e-mail header information may bring a message's authenticity into question.

Every decision related to the implementation and control of the e-mail system, its configuration and storage procedures, can impact e-mail's role as a convincing business record. Following a successful attack, e-mail may be excluded from evidence. A message's impact on proceedings may be severely diminished. Or the authenticity of every e-mail stored within an organization's system may be cast into doubt.

Real-Life E-Disaster Story: Poor Records Set Criminal Free

In overturning a criminal conviction, a court excluded computer evidence (though not e-mail) because it did not believe there was an adequate foundation for allowing bank e-records into evidence. The court was not convinced the records were made in the ordinary course of business, at or near the time the event was recorded, or that the information, method, and time of preparation were trustworthy.[2]

The Ordinary Course of Business

Thanks to an exception to the hearsay rule, business records normally may be used as evidence in court, provided that the records were created in the ordinary course of business. The courts' rationale: A record that is routinely and consistently created as the byproduct of a business activity is more likely to be trustworthy than a one-time record created for a specific purpose (in anticipation of litigation, for example).

Scenario: Imagine that your manufacturing company is sued by a customer claiming a shipment of parts was eight weeks late. The lawsuit alleges that the parts arrived at the customer's door twelve weeks after purchase, not four weeks as promised.

Litigation unearths an e-mail to the customer from one of your salespeople, promising delivery in twelve weeks. If you can

demonstrate that your sales team always e-mails order confir-
mations, as was done in this case, the court is more likely to
view this e-mail as trustworthy. On the other hand, if your salespeople have never before sent e-mails confirming purchases and
delivery dates, this e-mail may be viewed as suspicious. Perhaps
a company employee created the e-mail after the fact to fraudu-
lently influence the case.

Avoid similar scenarios by creating written policies, practices, and evidence of employee compliance related to e-mail use
as a real business tool.

What Makes Good E-Mail Business Records?

While e-mail often is admitted into evidence, there have been
numerous court cases in which e-mail has been attacked for not
satisfying the business records definition. In one case, the court
excluded an e-mail central to one party's legal position. The
court noted, "E-mail is far less of a systematic business activity
than a monthly inventory printout or other computer-generated
printout . . . e-mail is an on-going electronic message and retrieval system, whereas an electronic inventory recording system
is a regular, systematic function of a bookkeeper prepared in the
course of business."[3] Exclusion of the e-mail greatly diminished
the party's chances of prevailing.

In another case, however, e-mail messages in which a supervisor made sexual advances were allowed into evidence to prove
a sexual harassment claim.[4] In the context of a lawsuit, an
e-mail that is offered as evidence can be attacked for any number of reasons, including failure to satisfy the definition of a
business record. If it lacks the trust inherent in a standard business record, it won't be considered worthy of court acceptance
without additional proof that it's trustworthy.

Defense of Business Records Is a Time-Consuming Task

Ideally, all significant business content, regardless of form,
should be available and usable for litigation or other reasons. A
record with all the trappings of a business record may avoid

attack and enjoy business record status. Once a record is challenged, however, its legitimacy needs to be defended. Defending the use of company records is a time-consuming exercise. Productivity is wasted, money is spent, and frustration is likely, as the original drafter may no longer be available to testify.

Seven Ways to Bolster the Evidentiary Value of E-Mail Records

1. Develop rules for e-mail use. Let employees know what they may and may not say and do when it comes to business e-mail.

2. Advise employees that the organization's e-mail system exists exclusively for conducting and memorializing company business.

3. Establish guidelines for the proper e-mail documentation of business activities.

4. Create consistent patterns. If you send an e-mail to confirm every order placed and each delivery date promised, your e-mail making such delivery promises may be deemed trustworthy by the courts. You have demonstrated the use of confirming e-mail in the ordinary course of business.

5. Provide a list of "must have" content regarding the who, what, where, why, and when of e-mail. For example, if you always use your mail code in the signature block, its absence may suggest someone else sent an e-mail from your desk.

6. Develop security rules for system administrators.

7. Configure technology to maximize e-mail integrity and authenticity.

Self-Assessment: Business Evidence Risk Management

Using a scale of 1 to 5 (1 being the lowest, 5 the highest), answer each of the following questions about your organization's use of e-mail.

1. On average how would you rank the importance of transactions completed via
   e-mail?   1 2 3 4 5

2. How likely is it that an e-mail will be
   needed in the future for any business purpose?   1 2 3 4 5

3. What's the likelihood that you will need
   to use e-mail in a formal court proceeding?   1 2 3 4 5

4. What's the likelihood that required
   e-mail will not be readily available when
   needed?   1 2 3 4 5

5. Does your company fail to take e-mail
   management seriously?   1 2 3 4 5

What Your Responses Mean

If your responses total 15 or more, your organization needs to take e-mail management more seriously, and your e-risk management program may need work. Protect your legal interests by putting into place a strategic e-risk management program, complete with rules, policies, and procedures.

Recap and E-Action Plan:

E-Mail Rule #21: Manage E-Mail Business Records to Ensure Accuracy and Trustworthiness

1. Courts and regulators expect e-mail records to be complete, accurate, and trustworthy.

2. To use e-mail as evidence in a dispute, you may need to demonstrate the reliability of your e-mail system and messages.

3. Take the steps to bolster the evidentiary value of e-mail records.

CHAPTER 22

E-Mail Discovery
E-Mail Rule #22: Manage E-Mail in Anticipation of Litigation, Audits, and Investigations

As part of your organization's overall e-risk management strategy, it's essential to prepare for the day when your e-mail is requested in connection with an audit, investigation, arbitration, litigation, or other formal proceeding. E-mail and other forms of electronic communications are regularly targeted by litigators and investigators. Your system may be a treasure trove of information, which your opponent can use to bolster a case, embarrass your organization, or damage your reputation. Conversely, the e-mail in your system may protect your organization by advancing your legal position.

Why is e-mail so often used as a primary source of evidence in high-profile discrimination, sexual harassment, and antitrust litigation and claims? The casual nature of e-mail lulls even savvy users into a false sense of security. They mistakenly believe that they can use e-mail to say anything, without regard to context or reader interpretation. In addition, many users view e-mail as a private communication tool, regardless of written policy that clearly states that employees should not expect any privacy when using the organization's e-mail system.

Another problem stems from the fact that e-mail is so quick and easy to use. In seconds, messages can be written, transmitted, copied, printed, forwarded, pasted to other media, and circulated inside and outside your organization. This makes it next to impossible to control all potential sources of damaging or embarrassing content, not to mention tracking down all copies.

Assess Your Exposure to Litigation, Audits, and Investigations

1. Do employees retain e-mail on laptops, personal digital assistants, or desktop computers?
   (If yes, be aware that all these devices are potential discovery sources.) ___ Yes ___ No

2. Does e-mail exist on old backup tapes?
   (If yes, you may be required to duplicate and search through old backup tapes, even if you no longer own the software or hardware necessary to access the tapes.) ___ Yes ___ No

3. Do you allow employees to use alternative communication technology, such as voice mail, Instant Messaging, or discussion databases?
   (If yes, your electronic discovery challenge may not end with e-mail. Every form of electronic communication creates evidence that may be discoverable.) ___ Yes ___ No

4. Is the organization regularly involved in lawsuits or audits?
   (If yes, count on e-mail being used as evidence. Prepare today.) ___ Yes ___ No

5. Has your organization ever been party to a class-action lawsuit?
   (If yes, your e-mail system may be a primary target for litigators. You could be required to search thousands, even millions of potentially relevant e-mail messages.) ___ Yes ___ No

6. In the past decade, has your organization faced a governmental audit or investigation?
(If yes, expect future audits or investigations to call for the production of e-mail and other electronic records.)   __ Yes __ No

7. Does the organization apply retention rules to e-mail?
(If yes, your retention rules may come under scrutiny during a trial or audit. The court and auditors may inquire if e-mail records were kept for the right period of time, and they may question your decision to dispose of any e-mail records.)   __ Yes __ No

8. Does the technology department determine how long e-mail is stored on the organization's e-mail system?
(If yes, you are exposing yourself to e-disaster. Litigators could attack this practice, claiming decisions are driven by technology, not the law. The assumption: Your organization does not care sufficiently about its obligation to retain records and evidence.)   __ Yes __ No

9. Have employees been deposed during company-related litigation related to records, record keeping, company information management policy, or procedures?
(If yes, expect your e-mail management practices to be questioned or attacked. Litigators and investigators will search for flaws and weaknesses in your approach.)   __ Yes __ No

10. Does management control employees' e-mail content through policies, auditing, and monitoring?
(If no, could an opposing party use your

e-mail against you? Could your adversary locate messages in which employees discuss the organization's faulty products, incompetent employees, or inappropriate executive behavior?)   — Yes — No

11. Have employees ever been disciplined or fired for improper e-mail use?
(If yes, do you maintain complete and trustworthy records that reasonably prove that the dismissed employee was the perpetrator? Could someone else have sent the e-mail while the terminated employee's computer was unattended? You may need these records to defend your position.)   — Yes — No

What Is Discovery?

Discovery is the part of the litigation process in which opposing parties exchange relevant documents, testimony, and other information. Litigants generally request and receive information necessary to build a case in preparation for the trial. Discovery helps each side understand the material facts and evidence in advance of the trial. It also prevents anyone from being ambushed at the trial.

E-Mail's Role in Discovery

Increasingly, discovery is a battle itself, as litigants apply various discovery strategies to advance their cases. A belief among some litigators is that smoking gun e-mail should be pursued aggressively, as it likely will tip the legal scales in the discovering party's favor. In fact, e-mail has "become so commonplace that most court battles now involve discovery of some type of computer-stored information."[1]

According to the federal and state rules of evidence and civil procedure, discovery includes the production of electronic information. If you are involved in litigation, audits, investigations, and other formal proceedings, you must turn over all relevant information—e-mail and other forms—even if it hurts your legal position, embarrasses your organization, or devastates your case. Unfortunately, the business community often is poorly prepared and ill equipped to deal with electronic discovery. Adversaries gladly take advantage of the situation by targeting e-mail and other digital information for discovery.

E-Mail Discovery Challenges

1. Finding the storage media on which relevant messages may be located

2. Having the ability to search message content as well as the routing information

3. Reviewing all locations where e-mail may be located

4. Searching for responsive messages among the huge volume of messages

5. Needing special software or hardware to access a required message

6. Accessing other messages to create a contextual string

7. Accessing metadata and audit information related to a particular message

8. Accessing imbedded or linked information in the e-mail

What Organizations Are Required to Produce

Just about any tangible evidence or information in your possession or in the possession of your ASPs, records vendors, or other contracted service providers is potentially discoverable. Company e-mail or records at the ISP that provides you with Internet access and e-mail services may be fair game. E-material at the off-site storage facility provided by your records management vendor may be discoverable as well. E-mail located in enterprise servers across the country is discoverable. Old backup tapes, laptops, and handheld devices are all subject to discovery.

Rules of evidence and civil procedure have supported the discovery of electronic information for years. For example, in 1970 the Federal Rules of Civil Procedure (F.R.Civ.P.) were changed to account for electronic records. The rules define a discoverable document as including "writings, drawings, graphs, charts, photographs, phonorecords, and other data compilations from which information can be obtained, translated, if necessary, by the respondent through detection devices into reasonably usable form."[2] State rules relating to discovery contain similar language. Clearly, the broad definition of discoverable information applies not only to e-mail, but also to a wide range of electronic information.

Yet it may not be enough to produce e-mail evidence alone. According to the Federal Rules of Civil Procedure, litigants may be required to provide "a copy of, or a description by category and location of, all documents, data compilations, and tangible things that are in the possession, custody, or control of the party and that the disclosing party may use to support its claims or defenses."[3]

Failure to Produce Information

The courts have little patience with employers who claim they are unable to comply with broad e-mail discovery orders because of information system design flaws. After all, if a system is good enough to operate your business, it should be able to comply with the law. While courts consider time and cost when issuing discovery requests, genuine hardship can be difficult to prove. As one court put it, "If a party chooses to store information in a manner that tends to conceal rather than reveal, that party bears the burden of putting the information in a format useable by others."[4]

Because the courts have not taken a consistent approach in determining what is "unduly burdensome" or what efforts must be undertaken, predicting the outcome of a particular case is difficult. The bottom line is that e-mail discovery can burden organizations that have not implemented rules and invested in technology to retain and access required e-mail. It is in your organization's interests to develop and enforce e-mail rules that support your business, legal, and discovery needs.

Paper and Electronic Documents Must Be Produced

Certain types of data contain hidden information visible only in electronic form. For example, some word processing documents contain metadata (data about data) that provides information about authorship, editing, and document versioning. Courts may not be willing to accept hard copy if they suspect more or different information is available in the native digital format. As one court put it, "the law is clear that data in computerized form is discoverable even if paper 'hard copies' of the information have been produced. . . ."[5]

Spreadsheets include coded formulas that are intrinsic to the meaning of the data. E-mail is no different, in that the headers hold hidden information about authorship, origin, and routing, which may be integral to determining authenticity. Thus, courts in the past have required electronic versions of evidence be provided, even when printed copies were made available.[6]

If you are retaining e-mail by printing it to paper and then deleting the electronic version, it is in your best interests to ensure that comprehensive information about the e-mail and its attachments is printed, too.

E-Discovery Is Not Just About Litigation

The need to produce e-mail evidence is not limited to litigation. Increasingly organizations will be required to produce e-mail evidence for governmental investigations, compliance, and audits. In the regulatory world, executives have been penalized for their failure or lack of responsiveness, and companies have fallen for failing to protect important records.

In 2002, we witnessed unprecedented investigations of senior executives for violating company record-keeping requirements, failing to apply and enforce policies, and destroying records and other information.

One prominent executive was publicly arrested and indicted for obstruction of justice because he allegedly "directed another individual to . . . delete certain computer files . . . containing phone messages he received," even though he "well knew that at the time that he directed the destruction of documents . . . such documents were material to the SEC's investigation" regarding insider trading.[7]

The Food and Drug Administration (FDA) and other regulators expect information systems to be developed with ready access to electronic records and evidence in mind. FDA regulation 21 CFR Part 11 not only makes clear that records can be audited by the agency, but Section 11.10 (e) of the regulation also states that even the audit records for computer systems "shall be available for agency review and copying."

Similarly, the Securities and Exchange Commission (SEC) and National Association of Securities Dealers (NASD) regulations require brokerage companies to review and retain e-mail and make it available for regulatory review on relatively short notice. Recently, the SEC has been investigating several alleged violations at brokerage firms related to e-mail retention. Seven-figure fines potentially await the perpetrators.

Discovery of e-mail is not just about litigation. The FDA, the SEC, state insurance regulators, the IRS, and other regulators regularly request copies of, and in-house access to, e-mail and other e-records for audit or review. In light of the renewed vigor of audit and investigatory activities triggered by the financial scandals and executive misdeeds of 2002, an ounce of information management planning is worth its weight in gold.

Why Is E-Mail Such a Discovery Target?

Savvy litigators seek smoking gun e-mail for a number of reasons, including:

1. Most organizations lack e-mail management. Organizations rarely manage e-mail as they do other information. Mismanagement in the creation, transmission, storage, retention, and disposition process creates opportunities that litigators and investigators exploit. This increases the chance that there is a damaging message somewhere in e-mail sys-

tems, servers, networks, laptops, desktops, message pagers, PDAs, or backup tapes. Even if e-mail could or should have been disposed of long ago, there's still a chance one copy exists somewhere.

2. This court said it best in reference to a case where e-discovery turned into a battleground: "Neither the plaintiffs nor defendants have full command over what documents they possessed," even though the parties spent in excess of $1.5 million on discovery, an amount the court concluded was "nothing short of shocking" and "wholly disproportionate to what the evidence has disclosed."[8]

3. Producing unmanaged e-mail can be costly and inconvenient. E-discovery is used not only to gather information, but also to inconvenience opponents by making the process as time consuming and expensive as possible. Not that it takes much to inflict pain on organizations that fail to structure e-mail systems and develop policies to promote easy compliance with discovery orders.

4. Litigants have wasted millions of dollars and hundreds of hours searching for e-mail and other e-records, only to come up empty handed in some cases. Courts have held that searching e-mail messages is not "unduly burdensome" and sorting through employees' e-mail is necessary.

Sources of Discovery Cost

1. **Finding the right e-mail evidence.** Courts can and will burden organizations to search through vast amounts of e-mail for messages relevant to a case. One organization was required to search through 30 million pages of e-mail, at the company's own expense, for the names of particular individuals. The court found the costs for searching, compiling, formatting, and eliminating duplicates was not "unduly burdensome" because the difficulty and cost stemmed from the organization's own mismanagement and inadequate software.[9]

2. **Software development and purchase.** If your organization manages your e-mail in a proprietary, complex, or disorga-

nized format that would make it difficult to find and extract
messages relevant to a case, you might be "required to design a computer program to extract the data from its computerized business records, subject to the Court's discretion
as to the allocation of the costs of designing such a computer program."[10]

In other words, you may need to develop or purchase
software to enable your adversary to more easily access and
read your e-mail. In one case, an organization was required
to copy 210,000 pages of e-mail onto a hard drive in a
format the adversary could read. The organization previously had provided the e-mail on four-inch backup tapes,
which the adversary's hardware and software could not access.[11]

3. **Soft and hard costs.** Even simple operations like searching
through backup e-mail tapes can waste time and money.
Litigants routinely spend tens of thousands of dollars complying with e-discovery requests.

4. **Experts.** Forensic computer experts may be called in to find
and recover data from legacy systems and backup tapes or
to provide expert testimony. Technology experts may be
required to break codes and access proprietary systems or
to provide custom applications to opposing parties for access and retrieval. Experts also may be hired to develop
specialized programs for searching e-mail and other electronic information.

5. **Computing resources.** Your servers, desktop computers,
networks, and other devices may be taken offline or made
unavailable during e-discovery, requiring the purchase or
rental of additional systems. If electronic evidence is found
on media types your organization is no longer able to access, you could be required to purchase or rent legacy or
specialized equipment and software. You may even need to
employ technology experts if they are no longer employed
in-house.

6. **Lost productivity.** E-discovery typically eats into employees' productive time. This soft cost may be your greatest
source of expense, as IT professionals and other staff are

required to conduct searches and track down needed
e-records in the context of discovery. Productivity is lost as:

- Technology employees track down the locations of systems on which responsive e-mail may be located. And
  computer systems, including mainframes, networks,
  backup, and legacy systems are searched.

- Employees search the computers in their individual
  workspaces, including desktops, laptops, and PDAs.

Unmanaged E-Mail Is a Treasure Trove

Often the content found in unmanaged e-mail systems is damaging or embarrassing enough to compel a litigant to settle or
withdraw a case. Because casual conversations are commonly
memorialized through e-mail, Instant Messaging, and other
communication technologies, a funny or flippant comment can,
and all too often does, become Exhibit A in a lawsuit.

Smoking gun e-mail can be used to build a case, or it may
simply be found in your system in the course of discovery. If
you think you can protect yourself by selectively printing out
and handing over e-mail messages in response to a discovery
request, think again. The courts have required companies that
try this tactic to allow adversaries to search e-mail in its native
electronic format and on backup tapes to the extent that it exists.

Rather than trying to dodge a bullet, the best defense is to
apply the rules, policies, and practices discussed throughout this
book to ensure that damaging messages aren't written in the
first place, and nonrecord e-mail is regularly disposed of in the
ordinary course of business. The effect of following the rules is
that needed business e-mail is readily available and easier to
find because nonrecord e-mail has been deleted and is no longer
cluttering the storage device.

Contextual Concerns

E-mail and Instant Messages provide a special management
challenge because their contents are often contextual. Their
meaning may be linked to related messages in the chain of con-

versation, the reasoning behind the conversation, or the relationships that exist among the parties. Regardless, litigators may succeed in bolstering their cases by isolating individual messages.

Your organization's inability to separate e-mail and produce only relevant messages during discovery may cause so much embarrassment that management would opt to forgo litigation rather than face public ridicule. Failure to filter discoverable e-mail may result in evidence of sexual affairs, internal squabbling, and other embarrassing behavior being entered into the public record.

> "The real flaw is that the computer lies: It lies when it says DELETE."[12]

Without special software and processes, a "deleted" e-mail or Instant Message often is not really deleted. The file can remain accessible until the hard drive is overwritten with new data, which may never happen. Savvy litigants use this fact to their advantage at trials, retaining consultants who specialize in recovering "deleted" information for use in trial.

Compounding the deletion problem is the fact that it is extremely difficult to identify and manage all existing copies of messages and attachments. A single e-mail and its attachments may sit on the creator's computer, multiple e-mail servers, and the desktop, laptop, and handhelds of all recipients and elsewhere.

The best advice: Keep your content clean, your employees informed, and your rules up to date. Prevention, after all, is considerably less expensive than litigation.

Recap and E-Action Plan

E-Mail Rule #22: Manage E-Mail in Anticipation of Litigation, Audits, and Investigations

1. Locate and preserve all relevant e-mail and e-records as soon as you know they may be needed for litigation, audit, or investigation.

2. Make exact electronic copies of relevant e-mail and e-records. Put them in a segregated electronic archive.

3. Assign each case its own electronic file inside the segregated electronic archive established for discovery purposes.

4. Place electronic archives where they can easily be found.

5. Retain the original electronic version of responsive (related to the proceeding) e-mail or e-records for the duration of a lawsuit, audit, or investigation.

6. Label your electronic archive and contents appropriately. Include the case name and caption, names of parties, file date, responsible attorney, "privileged and confidential" coding, etc.

7. Make sure the discovery archive of responsive material includes nothing outside the scope of the discovery in the case. Anything contained in the segregated case archive may be reviewed by your adversary.

8. Control access to electronic copies of responsive e-mail or e-records to minimize attacks on their trustworthiness and credibility.

9. If you use your systems to show your opponent e-records in electronic form, be sure that the location and computer used do not allow access to unrelated data.

CHAPTER 23

Destruction of Evidence
E-Mail Rule #23: It's Illegal to Destroy E-Mail Evidence After You Have Received Notice of a Lawsuit or During a Trial

Common sense and the law may forbid the destruction of evidence and information before or during trial, but that doesn't stop it from happening, often triggering dire consequences. Employees who destroy e-mail and other evidence before or during formal proceedings place the organization and themselves at risk. Both civil and criminal penalties (including imprisonment) have resulted from destruction of evidence, or "spoliation," as it is called in the legal context.[1]

To quote one court: "A party is obligated to retain evidence that it knows or reasonably should know may be relevant to pending or future litigation. . . . Obviously service of a discovery demand places a party on notice to preserve the materials explicitly requested, but the duty to preserve arises whenever a party has been served with a complaint or anticipates litigation."[2]

Potential Penalties for Destroying Evidence

1. You are fined and must pay monetary damages.

2. You lose the case.

3. The court allows the jury to draw negative inferences from your action.

4. You may face a separate lawsuit for destruction of evidence.

5. There are other criminal or civil penalties.

Ensuring the Preservation of Evidence

Every organization needs a "records hold" mechanism to ensure that required records and other evidence of all formats and types are preserved in the context of imminent or pending litigation, audits, investigations, and other formal proceeding. Through a documented process, you must inform affected employees, executives, and administrators of their obligation to find, preserve, and produce required evidence, records, and other information.

Take the 2002 Arthur Andersen case, in which the consulting firm was found guilty of destroying records related to its client Enron, the target of a federal investigation. One of the central figures in the records destruction allegations was a partner who apparently thought it was all right to dispose of records according to the retention schedule, as long as the firm had not yet been subpoenaed or received notice of a congressional investigation into Enron's accounting practices.

The partner apparently believed working papers and other Enron-related documents (which would have been disposed of in the ordinary course of business had Arthur Andersen employees followed policy) could be destroyed in spite of indications they might have been relevant to the government's investigation. Wrong. The partner's inappropriate destruction of business records, including e-mail, helped cast the consulting firm in a particularly unfavorable light and contributed to Arthur Andersen's eventual downfall.[3]

The lesson: If you haven't followed your own policies, and you suspect your organization is in trouble, it's already too late. Implement and enforce records management policies before disaster strikes. Never rush to dispose of records and other information once you have reason to believe your organization will be party to a lawsuit, investigation, or audit.

Self-Erasing or Self-Destructing E-Mail with Encryption

In response to the business community's ardent wish that damaging e-mail would just disappear, a host of vendors have emerged in the past few years claiming they can do just that. The manufacturers of self-erasing or self-destructing e-mail assert that they can help prevent sensitive e-mail from falling into the wrong hands, being forwarded to competitors, or surfacing during litigation.

Typically, e-mail messages are encrypted, complete with an expiration date that ensures that messages can be read or accessed for a set period of time only. The same technology can be used to control who accesses a message and whether they can forward, change, or print the message.

The problem is that in a legal setting, a court or judge may have trouble accepting the fact that the interests of an opposing party in a trial cannot be served because of difficulties or expenses related to recovering encrypted messages. Furthermore, using technology that deliberately shrouds information could be interpreted as an attempt to hide evidence and obstruct justice.

While this technology certainly may have utility, be aware that self-erasing/self-destructing e-mail may come complete with its own brand of legal problems. Consult your attorney and assess all the business benefits and legal risks before taking advantage of this technology.

Recap and E-Action Plan

E-Mail Rule #23: It's Illegal to Destroy E-Mail Evidence After You Have Received Notice of a Lawsuit or During a Trial

1. Employees who destroy e-mail and other evidence after they know about a lawsuit or investigation, or during formal proceedings, put the organization at risk of civil and criminal penalties.

2. You are obligated to retain evidence that's likely to be relevant to pending or imminent litigation.

3. Establish a "records hold" mechanism to ensure that required records and other evidence of all formats and types are preserved.

4. Implement and enforce records management policies before disaster strikes.

5. Self-erasing/self-destructing e-mail may create legal problems, so assess the risks before using the technology.

CHAPTER 24

Discovery Rules for Employees
E-Mail Rule #24: E-Discovery Is Inevitable—Be Prepared

After learning of the Enron investigation (see previous chapter), had Arthur Andersen's senior management notified affected employees of their obligation to preserve relevant information, no matter how damaging or embarrassing, the case might have turned out differently. If records were destroyed, the firm could have argued that the destruction was the work of a rogue employee operating alone. Penalties might have been doled out, but the company might not have suffered irreparable damage. Perhaps Andersen's assets, clients, and reputation could have been preserved.

The law aside, there is a certain futility to destroying electronic evidence. The probability that every incriminating e-mail on the server, backup tapes, computers, and devices can be found and destroyed is slim. The only thing likely to be accomplished is the creation of clear evidence that you broke the law by destroying evidence. To ensure that everyone in your organization understands that fact, follow these steps:

1. **Give employees written rules to follow.** At the first sign your organization may be involved in a lawsuit, investigation, or audit, advise affected employees of their responsi-

bilities and what action should, and should not, be taken. That includes:

a. Searching through locally stored e-mail for relevant messages and all records, electronic records, documents, and information; searching responsive e-mail based on your adversary's name, the product at issue, the employee(s) involved, previous complaints, and so on.

   The scope of the search may differ for each employee, depending on the employee's role in the company and relationship to the litigation. In a product liability dispute, for example, the e-mail records of a product designer may contain more relevant information than those of a sales representative, depending on the nature of the dispute.

b. Searching through local file folders and cabinets for printouts of responsive e-mail and attachments. If the organization's practice is to retain e-mail in this manner, then include printed material in the search. Employees may be holding electronic and printed copies of relevant e-mail that's in need of preservation.

c. Copying and turning over relevant e-mail messages to the legal department.

d. Providing company lawyers with information about specific e-mail records and explaining the context of an employee's involvement in relevant issues. Pay special attention to e-mail and other electronic information. If your organization has policies that require the disposition of all e-mail at short intervals, then special measures may be necessary to ensure that required e-mail is preserved manually or at the central server. Consider issuing special notices to employees and administrators addressing e-mail records' retention and preservation.

2. **Document and preserve proof of notification and other actions.** It's important your organization creates and retains proof that e-discovery-related policies were in place and required actions were taken. This may be as simple as keeping a copy of a printed letter and a list of the offices it was delivered to. Or it may be as complex as keeping digital records of system access and other activities indicating em-

ployee actions. Consider installing software to help demonstrate employees received and read e-mail notices of their responsibilities.

3. **Ensure that the production process is trustworthy.** The process you use to collect required e-mail and other relevant information should not open you to claims that it may have been altered in the process. A documented process for employees to find, copy, and otherwise produce needed information will be beneficial. Also, technology is now available to "freeze" e-records, pre-empting claims that records were tampered with after they were found and produced.

Recap and E-Action Plan
E-Mail Rule #24: E-Discovery Is Inevitable—Be Prepared

1. Retain e-mail according to retention rules.

2. Dispose of e-mail and other material according to company policy. Keeping information longer only creates greater expense and potential liability.

3. Retain records only in the authorized paper or electronic medium.

4. Organize e-mail records like all other paper records.

5. Label folders properly for contents.

6. Protect privileged and confidential material.

7. Never keep convenience, or unofficial, copies longer than necessary.

8. Never retain convenience copies longer than the retention policy dictates for official copies.

9. Do not keep multiple copies of the same e-mail.

10. Do not store e-mail on separate computers or in separate locations.

11. Keep only e-mail records. Dispose of duplicates, drafts, and nonrecords immediately when they are no longer needed.

CHAPTER 25

Creating an E-Discovery Response Strategy
E-Mail Rule #25: Plan Today to Meet the Challenges of Litigation, Audits, and Investigations Tomorrow

If you have not yet dealt with the challenges of finding and producing e-mail evidence for litigation, audits, and investigations, consider yourself lucky. You have the opportunity to prepare for the inevitable and get it right.

Are You Prepared for E-Discovery?

If required, could you accomplish the following, and be confident of doing a thorough job, in just a few short weeks?

1. Search the past five years' worth of e-mail and discussion databases for messages containing a specific employee's name   __ Yes __ No

2. Search all e-mail on laptops, desktops, and PDAs for East Coast regional sales

data contained within messages or attachments.   ___ Yes   ___ No

3. Locate log files and audit entries for all unauthorized attempts to access or hack into your e-mail system in the last two years.   ___ Yes   ___ No

4. Find Instant Messages and e-mail in which twelve named employees' job performances are appraised.   ___ Yes   ___ No

5. Locate copies of Web pages and Web log records from any company Web site that was online on November 11, 2002, and could have been or was viewed by a specific named company prior to its entering into a transaction with you.   ___ Yes   ___ No

6. Search for e-mail comments and discussion from 1997 to the present, regarding accounting practices and allocation of expenses.   ___ Yes   ___ No

7. Search all computers for e-mail messages, attachments, copies, drafts, and duplicates relating to a specific contract. Identify the location of each.   ___ Yes   ___ No

8. Search the e-mail system for metadata and audit trail records related to a January 15, 2002, e-mail transmitted by a specific named individual.   ___ Yes   ___ No

9. Locate e-mail, Instant Messaging, chat, or discussion database comments made by product design team members suggesting an air freshener canister they developed is prone to explode.   ___ Yes   ___ No

10. Find cookie files on the desktop and laptop computers of all male supervisors in the field audit team.   ___ Yes   ___ No

If you answered yes to all of the above, you have learned your lessons well. You are prepared to respond to an e-discovery request. Even one no answer, however, means you need to start planning today to meet the challenges of litigation, audits, and investigations, as early as tomorrow.

Recap and E-Action Plan

E-Mail Rule #25: Plan Today to Meet the Challenges of Litigation, Audits, and Investigations Tomorrow

1. **Be proactive.** Litigators hope you are sitting idle, ill prepared for problems. Undermine the opposition's litigation strategy by having your discovery plan in place and ready to go.

2. **Assign clear responsibilities.** Every executive and employee in your organization should clearly understand e-discovery responsibilities. The courts have chided executives and directors for not assuming an active oversight role in e-discovery. Policy development, training, enforcement, notification, and related tasks should be assigned, managed, and completed.[1]

3. **Train employees.** Be sure employees understand IT challenges from management's perspective. Audit employees' actions against related policies. Inform employees of their obligation to manage records and other information in accordance with written policies. Explain organizational and individual obligations in the face of audits, investigations, and litigation.

4. **Install the right technology.** Install management and searching tools to facilitate your search and production of e-mail required for discovery. The more easily and accurately you can search e-mail by keywords, routing information, dates, names, and subject lines, the more likely you will respond to discovery requests quickly and inexpensively. Technology should offer flexibility in search and retrieval, yet ensure the trustworthy completion of tasks. Discovery needs are served, and business goals supported.

5. **Establish a records hold mechanism.** Employees who control information related to an audit, investigation, or litigation must be notified of their responsibilities. E-mail that normally would be disposed of in the ordinary course of business pursuant to a retention schedule, for example, now may have to be retained in anticipation of litigation.

6. **Use native or electronic format.** Maintaining e-mail messages in their native or electronic format eases searching for and producing relevant e-mail. The courts have required employers to provide electronic copies of e-mail messages even though hard copies already were submitted. The courts do not look kindly on organizations that attempt to undercut an adversary.

   One organization tried to meet its discovery obligation by giving its adversary access to dozens of international warehouses in which paper records were stored, even though the same records were available in a database. The court ruled that the organization failed to fulfill the requirements of the Federal Rules of Civil Procedure, which require documents be available for inspection at a reasonable place. The court considered the organization's act an "empty gesture . . . arguably designed to further frustrate the discovery process."[2]

7. **Move data to inactive systems.** If discovery involves relevant e-mail messages and other information on active servers, networks, and desktop computers, these devices will need to be accessed during the discovery process. Endeavor to move e-mail and other electronic records off active systems and onto records management systems. Doing so not only frees up computer resources, but also may bolster the trustworthiness of digital information by moving it out of the hands of the drafter.

8. **Insist on IT participation.** Your IT department "owns" the systems that create, manage, and store e-mail. IT should be part of e-discovery planning and execution. Work with IT to ensure that information technology is purchased and installed with e-discovery goals in mind. Involve IT staff in training executives and attorneys, searching and producing e-mail, and providing testimony and related information.

9. **Audit, enforce, and retrain.** Policies are only as good as your employees' ability to understand and comply with them. Require employee signatures on policies as an acknowledgement of their awareness and understanding of the rules and the penalties for noncompliance. Records created and kept in the ordinary course of business can be used to demonstrate that your company and its employees acted appropriately. They also can help insulate the company from the bad acts of employees.

10. **Designate an e-mail czar.** Having a technology or information security expert oversee the search and production of e-mail helps ensure that consistent procedures are followed and employee participation is taken seriously. Remember to document your search so that you and your adversary know what has been searched and what has not been.

PART FIVE
E-Mail Security

CHAPTER 26

E-Mail Security

E-Mail Rule #26: Develop Policies and Procedures to Secure E-Mail

If you think the topic of computer security is just for techno wizards and computer nerds, think again. Computer security plays an important role in keeping your e-mail system safe and secure and keeping your organization out of legal hot water.

Good e-mail business records are not made by accident. Implementation of an e-mail system and the development of e-mail policies and practices take careful planning. Even seemingly innocuous e-mail activity can create liability, risk, and expense.

System Configuration

The same features that make life easier for e-mail users also can create legal hardships for employers. Imagine, for example, that a vice president sends an e-mail to managers stating, "I think Mary's career goals could be achieved if she took a more active role in managing the junior members of her team."

A disgruntled manager alters the message and distributes it companywide. The altered e-mail reads, "I think Mary's career goals could be realized if she hiked up her skirt a bit." In the ensuing discrimination lawsuit for gender bias, the altered e-mail will be central to Mary's case. Considerable time and money will be spent trying to prove what really happened, who was involved, and when it occurred.

Information Security

Scenario: In early 2000, the HR department receives an e-mail from Jeff, an employee, requesting that all his retirement money be invested in a technology stock fund offered by the company. At his direction, the retirement accounts manager moves the $50,000 Jeff had accumulated in a money market fund over the past two decades into a technology stock fund.

Months go by, and Jeff forgets about the change. Statements arrive in the mail, but he doesn't open them for eighteen months. When he finally looks at a monthly statement, he's horrified to see his account has plummeted to $13,400.

Jeff contacts the HR department the next day to report a mistake: "My statement indicates I have a technology investment, but I don't invest in technology. This is a huge mistake that needs to be corrected immediately."

The HR manager promises to look into the matter. Three days later, Jeff is informed that the investment option on his retirement account was changed on April 17, 2000, in response to Jeff's e-mail request. Jeff counters that he never sent the e-mail, and he questions how the organization knows he did.

Next Jeff receives a call from a supervisor explaining the e-mail was sent from Jeff's desktop computer to HR. Although the organization has routing information and the original e-mail to prove Jeff originated the message, he doesn't waiver.

Jeff files suit. The case hinges on how long an e-mail account stays active after an employee stops using it. Security surrounding passwords and unique IDs also is at issue.

During discovery, Jeff's attorneys learn a 14-person department has access to all passwords and IDs used by employees at Jeff's division. At headquarters, on the other hand, passwords and IDs are controlled by two different units. (Clearly, the way passwords are managed at headquarters is more secure. No one person knows an employee's password and unique ID. Plus, few employees have access to that type of information to begin with.) Management's failure to secure passwords and IDs at Jeff's division may provide Jeff with the argument that a malicious security unit employee sent the erroneous e-mail from Jeff's computer workstation.

Virus Attacks

To: bill@recipient.net
From: allisonm@sender.net

Subject: Worm Klez.E immunity
Klez.E is the most common worldwide spreading worm. Very dangerous, it corrupts your files.
Because of its stealth and antiantivirus technique, most common antivirus software can't detect or clean it.
We developed this free immunity tool to defeat the malicious virus.
You only need to run this tool once, and Klez will never enter your PC.
NOTE: Because this tool acts as a fake Klez to fool the real worm, your antivirus software may scream when you run it.
Ignore the warning and select "continue."
If you have any questions, please mail to me.

Despite the helpful tone, taking the action outlined in this real e-mail message will ensure your computer is infected with the Klez virus. Adding insult to injury, if you click on "mail to me," the message will be forwarded to another victim, not the originator of the virus.

Consider the Legal Risks

As illustrated by these three examples, the e-mail world is a security minefield. From viruses attacking your system, to hackers defacing your Web sites, to intruders using your computer to launch attacks on other organizations, to malicious employees stirring up internal strife and external litigation, to the theft of confidential information—the stakes are high.

Consider the legal risks, too. What if a careless employee e-mails a patient's confidential medical records to the wrong patient? Are there legal consequences if, because you failed to update your virus protection, a virus spreads to every employee's address book and attacks thousands of recipients' e-mail systems? What if a desperate employee, facing divorce and financial ruin, uses your computer system to hack into a competitor's system and embezzle funds?

Anticipating and addressing these and other security disasters before they strike will help you minimize risks and losses.

Develop an Information Security Strategy

Failing to secure business information, including e-mail, exposes your organization to numerous risks:

- Information is corrupted or lost.

- Data is misappropriated and misused.

- Systems fail, and business is interrupted.

- Corporate reputations are ruined.

- Integrity of information assets is jeopardized.

- Property and assets are stolen.

- Business transactions are disrupted and relationships tarnished.

- Customer privacy is violated.

- Productivity declines.

- Business records—including proprietary information, trade secrets, privileged and confidential communications—are tampered with.

Seven Secrets of E-mail Security

1. Perfect security does not exist.
2. The bad acts of good employees can decimate great security.
3. The real security work begins after technology is purchased.
4. There is more than one way to secure e-mail.
5. Different security issues require different solutions.
6. Money alone can't solve security problems.
7. Security is more than firewalls and encryption.

Security Is a Process

Thanks to headline news coverage of security breaches, a proliferation of security-oriented software, and the emergence of security as a competitive feature in enterprise software, most organizations are heavily invested in security technology. Unfortunately, too many organizations sit back and relax once they have added the latest software and hardware for access controls, encryption, antivirus, and firewalls.

This is a big mistake. Security is a process that demands constant vigilance. Failure to properly maintain, configure, and update technology can defeat your entire security system.

New viruses invade the e-world daily. Failure to regularly update antivirus software makes you vulnerable to attack. Ditto for internal hackers and malicious intruders. All it takes is a momentary lapse to bring your organization, now totally reliant on e-mail, to a standstill.

A Cost-Benefit Approach to Risk

Nearly 90 percent of organizations today assign responsibility for connecting security efforts to business risks, up from just 30 percent in 2001.[1]

Risk factors to consider:

- How much money or information is at risk in any given e-mail transaction?
- What damage could result from a security breach?
- What's the likelihood of a security breach?
- Do you need to protect confidential, private, or privileged information?
- How motivated are outsiders to access your information?

The amount of time and money your organization invests in security should be commensurate with the risks. It is a simple cost-benefit analysis.

Assess Your Organization's E-Mail Security Risks and Needs

1. Do you prohibit sending confidential information via unencrypted e-mail? ___ Yes ___ No

2. Do company rules require employees to secure their e-mail mailboxes? ___ Yes ___ No

3. Does the company expect to protect personal or private information about individuals or organizations? ___ Yes ___ No

4. Has any employee ever transmitted an e-mail to the wrong recipient? ___ Yes ___ No

5. Has your e-mail system ever been attacked by viruses it could not stop from damaging the network or computer workstations? ___ Yes ___ No

6. Do you know how long it takes to deactivate an unattended e-mail account? ___ Yes ___ No

7. Have employees been trained on e-mail system password management? ___ Yes ___ No

8. Has anyone ever used another employee's e-mail account without authorization? ___ Yes ___ No

9. Has anyone ever received a virus via an e-mail attachment? ___ Yes ___ No

10. Can employees access the organization's e-mail system from remote locations? ___ Yes ___ No

What Your Responses Mean

If you answered yes to any of these questions, your organization likely has e-mail security needs that must be addressed before disaster strikes.

Information Security Is a Corporate Governance Issue

Scenario: A manufacturer was engaged in a multi-billion-dollar redesign of its product line. The top-secret project was expected to bury the competition and propel the manufacturer to the top of its industry. The project was proceeding smoothly, until an employee stole and leaked details to an unauthorized Web site. With the program compromised, the manufacturer had nothing to show for its enormous expenditure of cash, time, and talent—a waste that could have been prevented or minimized had the organization taken precautions to block unauthorized access and data theft. Adding insult to injury, the security failure triggered several lawsuits.

Laws Mandating Security

Increasingly, the laws governing e-mail and other e-records make it clear that legally sufficient records call for secure storage and management, from creation to use. Some laws even spell out exactly how to create a secure e-system and deliver a trustworthy business record.

For example, the pharmaceutical industry regulation dealing with electronic records specifies the use of "secure, computer-generated, time-stamped audit trails to independently record the time and date of operator entries and actions that create, modify, or delete electronic records. Record changes shall not obscure previously recorded information. Such audit trail documentation shall be retained as long as that required for the subject electronic records and shall be available for agency review and copying."[2]

The FDA regulation continues by mandating the use of "authority checks to ensure that only authorized individuals can use the system, electronically sign a record, access the operation or computer system input or output device, alter a record, or perform the operation at hand."[3]

The message is clear: Build and monitor secure systems that ensure content is unaltered from creation until disposition.

Recap and E-Action Plan

E-Mail Rule #26: Develop Policies and Procedures to Secure E-Mail

1. Computer security helps keep your e-mail system safe and secure and can help protect your organization.

2. The e-mail world is a security minefield full of business and legal risks.

3. Security is an ongoing process that requires constant vigilance.

4. The amount of time and money invested in security should be commensurate with the risks.

5. Adhere to industry regulations that govern security.

CHAPTER 27

Physical and Network Security

E-Mail Rule #27: Strategic E-Mail Security Involves Physical and Network Security

Physical Security

The goal of physical security is simple: limit physical access to your in-house information systems by employees and outsiders. That includes e-mail. To that end, develop information security rules that clearly delineate who is allowed physical access to server rooms, data centers, and other locations housing hardware and software.

Damage to enterprise systems often comes from within. All it takes is one disgruntled employee with unfettered access in order to severely damage data, computers, reputations, and pocketbooks. Unauthorized insider access has cost business as much as $50 million annually, according to the CSI and FBI.[1] Can you afford to lose even a fraction of that amount?

Enhance your physical security strategy by limiting physical access solely to employees who are responsible for maintaining and operating systems. And don't forget to train IT personnel to treat their access rights with care.

Controlling Physical Security with IDs and Passwords

Use IDs to manage employee security clearance and keep unauthorized persons out.

Passwords tend to be treated far too freely in many organizations. Enhance security by requiring employees to follow these passwords procedures:

1. Use at least eight characters.

2. Combine upper- and lowercase letters with numbers.

3. Steer clear of the obvious—names of kids, spouses, pets, etc.

4. Keep passwords hidden, not taped to computer monitors or stashed in desk drawers.

Stay Current

One important maintenance function of system administrators and information security professionals is ensuring that employee IDs and passwords are current. As job functions shift and access changes, IDs and passwords need to change. As employees are promoted, transferred, or terminated, their access rights, IDs, and passwords must be adjusted. And don't forget to change passwords and IDs organizationwide following layoffs, downsizing, or any event likely to create hard feelings or trigger acts of revenge among employees.

Real-Life E-Disaster Stories: Password Problems

While auditing its information security program, the management of one very embarrassed organization learned that hundreds of former workers (including terminated employees) still had remote access to the e-mail system. While policy and procedures were in place to remove users from the authorized list as soon as their employment ended, management had failed to take the rule seriously or follow through.

In another case, which is now winding through the courts, an employer sued an ex-employee for retaining former colleagues' e-mail addresses and communicating with them after leaving the company. When the ex-employee refused to stop e-mailing the organization's employees, management sued. The unique legal grounds: The ex-employee was trespassing on the organization's personal property.

Clearly, filing suit against all your former employees would be a huge waste of time as well as a financial drain. Be proactive. As part of your security policy or information ownership policy, make it clear that the organization, not the individual, owns e-mail addresses and passwords. Require employees to turn over all copies of in-house e-mail address directories and passwords (their own, as well as other employees') at the time of termination (voluntary or involuntary) or retirement.

Physical Access Considerations

As part of your overall security strategy, be sure to have your information security people assess and address physical security in and around your organization.

- Is intrusion detection and monitoring in place?

- Who has access to buildings?

- Who has access to computer rooms?

- Are at least two system administrators required to change, alter, or modify the e-mail server settings?

- Who has access to storage media containing company information?

- Who has access to employees' computers?

- Who has access to third-party facilities and systems storing your organization's business records?

- Who interacts with storage and records vendors? Limit access to limit risk.

- Has the organization implemented stringent rules of access? Are universal codes or keys, IDs, and passwords used to access computers and facilities?

Network Security and E-Mail

Network security includes the e-mail system's internal network, along with the connections to the Internet and alternative electronic communications tools. Approach network security with the assumption that any e-mail message can be read by anyone at any time, unless you take specific measures to protect it.

You want to control access to your internal networks and content. For example, if the engineering group uses e-mail or a discussion database on the network to communicate about the top-secret product they are working on, you must establish rules and controls governing who may access that content collection. Even system administrators, who otherwise have access to the entire system, may be banned from certain highly confidential information.

Firewalls Close the Internal Network's Door

Firewalls are a standard tool for securing the perimeter around internal networks. A firewall simply controls the traffic on the network. Firewalls are designed to keep your organization separated from the fire of hackers, viruses, and other security threats. Just remember that a firewall is only as good as its implementation, configuration, and maintenance.

Recap and E-Action Plan

E-Mail Rule #27: Strategic E-Mail Security Involves Physical and Network Security

1. Update network access security codes regularly—daily, if necessary.

2. Make sure employees have network access on an as-needed basis only.

3. Limit the number of employees with system administrator access.

4. Give network administrators guidelines for the proper use of network access.

5. Establish rules for employee password creation, maintenance, and protection.

6. Have information security, e-mail administrators, and business units develop a simple mechanism to ensure that changes in employee status are communicated in a timely fashion to the unit responsible for changing access controls.

7. Following termination, transfer, or retirement, employees' e-mail account content should be controlled by their supervisors.

8. The contents of employees' e-mail accounts belong to the organization and should be reviewed at the time of any employee's departure.

9. Protect against employees transferring company information or customer lists via e-mail by auditing and monitoring e-mail files as soon as you learn of an employee's plan to leave the organization.

CHAPTER 28

Content Security—Inbound
E-Mail Rule #28: Inbound Message and Attachment Content Is Critical to E-Mail Security

In addition to securing your e-mail system's physical locations, computers, and components, you also need to develop a security strategy covering e-mail message and attachment content. Content security policies work hand in hand with written e-mail rules and policies to protect the organization from inappropriate, confidential, or abusive messages traveling into or out of your system.

According to IDC research, worldwide e-mail use will soar to 35 billion messages a day by 2005.[1] With that amount of activity, your organization must put a strategic content security program in place as part of your overall e-risk management strategy.

Controlling Inbound Information

Establish and enforce a content security program designed to:

■ Ensure that viruses, Trojan horses, and worms stay outside the firewall.

■ Keep inappropriate, offensive content out of your system.

■ Prevent oversized attachments from crippling your system.

■ Keep videos, music, and other nonessential resource-intensive content out.

■ Battle spam.

■ Screen and/or capture discussion database messages.

Support the Integrity of E-Mail

Use your content security policy to demonstrate to courts, regulators, and auditors that your retained business e-mail is trustworthy.

■ Make sure you can prove e-mail has not been altered, from the time of creation to the present.

■ Capture enough audit information to identify message senders and receivers.

■ Be prepared to show transmission and receipt times.

■ Retain and be ready to display the complete content of an e-mail record, including attachments and embedded information.

■ Demonstrate system integrity with metadata and audit trails.

Apply the Three Es of Risk Management

Maximize the effectiveness of your content security program by focusing on the three Es of e-mail risk management: (1) *establish* e-mail policy; (2) *educate* employees; and (3) *enforce* rules to guarantee the integrity of stored messages. That calls for teamwork on the part of your legal counsel, HR manager, IT department, employees, and content security software vendor.

Inbound Risks: Viruses, Worms, Trojan Horses, and Other Malicious Code

The primary job of content security is ensuring that all inbound and outbound e-mail is secure and trustworthy. That brings us to a discussion of the 1,000-pound gorilla of content security: the virus.

Ideally, most viruses will be stopped by firewall protection and blocked from entering the secure internal company network. If a virus does get through, however, your e-mail rules and policies should provide employees with the tools necessary to help stop it in its tracks.

What Makes Viruses Such a Threat to Security?

A virus is computer code or a program designed to create mischief, intrude, exploit, or harm the computing environments used by and within most organizations. Viruses typically enter computers through e-mail attachments. When the attachment is opened, the virus is executed and gains access to the network. Viruses are continually altering themselves to prevent detection.

Unless you know exactly what an attachment contains or can verify that it comes from a reliable source, its contents could contain a virus. Viruses usually are the handiwork of individuals with no specific motivation for attacking a particular person or organization (unlike hackers). Rather, people who send viruses tend to be motivated by the desire to cause a commotion.

Sophisticated viruses target programs that grab contact directories and, in turn, use the victim's e-mail address book and account to further spread the virus. Damage is widespread and rapid, as the virus uses your contact list to self-propagate. Your contacts feel safe opening e-mail that comes from you. In so doing, they expose their contacts to the same virus, which may spread unfettered around the world, until it is finally quarantined.

If a self-propagating virus uses your address book as its jumping-off point, you are at risk on two levels. When you explain the situation to everyone in your e-mail address book, you risk damaging business relationships. In addition, you face the risk of being sued for failing to detect the virus and allowing it to infect other organizations' systems.

As if self-propagating viruses aren't bad enough, business is also at risk from virus hoaxes. Variations on "standard" viruses, a virus hoax e-mail might ask the reader to take a specific action related to a file already contained in the recipient's system. The hoax message might claim a virus is living in your system now, and—in order to rid yourself of it—you must locate and delete a file with an "exe" suffix. Only after you delete the file as instructed do you learn it was critical to your system. Without the .exe file, your system fails.

Trojan Horses, Worms, Denial of Service Attacks, and Sniffers

A Trojan horse is a malicious code that sneaks in via an e-mail attachment and waits to take action in the future. Its main objective is to get into your computer and lie in wait, rather than disrupt computer function today.

Similar to a virus, a worm attacks the computer and network storage to disrupt the system.

A denial of service attack is a malicious way to interrupt service, prohibit authorized users from accessing or using the system, or ruin part of the system—just for "fun."

Cyberspace is populated by technically savvy people who spend their days grabbing information from the Internet in the hopes it will be useful and profitable. Sophisticated information "packet sniffers," intent on corporate espionage and property theft, grab sensitive and proprietary information sent out of protected corporate and institutional environments. Your loss is their gain, as they benefit from your confidential data, classified information, and customer account numbers.

Stop Attacks in Their Tracks

While you cannot stop malicious intruders from attacking your system, you can take steps to ensure that the resulting damage is kept to a minimum. Start with employee education. A few tips:

■ Never open e-mail attachments from senders you don't recognize.

■ Even if you know the sender, don't open an attachment with an odd or "off" name without first calling the sender to verify that the message and attachment are legitimate.

■ Before opening any attachment, scan for viruses. If there is a virus present, quarantine it.

■ To succeed in causing mischief, viruses usually require executable programs. Before opening any attachment with an ".exe" suffix (executable), look for clues that a virus may be present. If you have any doubt, do not open the attachment.

Spotting Clues to Detect Viruses

Imagine that you have received the following e-mail from a family member. What clues, if any, would make you hesitate to open it?

> To: louieshooter@recipient.spike
> From: stanleyshooter@sender.spike
> Subject: IReallyLoveYou
> Take a look at the attached. You will really love it.
> Attachment: IReallyLoveYou.exe

Analysis: Before opening any attachment, look closely at the message for clues about its legitimacy. Remember, most viruses have to "execute" in order to create problems. The message itself rarely contains a virus.

This message contains several clues:

■ When was the last time your brother sent a message with a subject stating "I Really Love You"? If he's never sent a message with this type of subject line, you have good reason to confirm whether or not it was sent by your brother. If it wasn't, it could contain a virus or other malicious code.

■ Does your brother usually personalize his e-mail with a salutation (Dear Lou) or personalization in the body (Louie)? If so, the absence of a salutation or personalization should alert you to a problem.

■ Why is there no signature ("Stanley" or "S") or close ("Talk to you next week")?

■ Would your brother ever send an attachment with such a strange name?

■ Always check .exe attachments for viruses.

Other clues that should make you pause before download-ing a message without first verifying its true origin and contents:

■ Virus is mentioned in the subject line.

■ Action is requested in the subject line.

■ Extreme importance is indicated in the subject line.

■ It's doubtful your contact would share the information con-tained.

Recap and E-Action Plan

E-Mail Rule #28: Inbound Message and Attachment Content Is Critical to E-Mail Security

1. It's essential to develop a security strategy covering in-bound e-mail messages and content.

2. Content security policies work with written e-mail rules and policies to keep inappropriate, confidential, or abusive messages from traveling into and out of your organization.

3. Use your content security policy to demonstrate to courts, regulators, and auditors that your organization's e-mail is trustworthy.

4. Educate employees about attachment risks. Provide guide-lines for opening or quarantining attachments.

CHAPTER 29

Content Security—Outbound
E-Mail Rule #29: Outbound E-Mail Is Critical to E-Mail Security

Employers face a whole host of content security issues that have nothing to do with attacks from malicious outsiders. Rather, they concern inappropriate and offensive e-mail content (written and transmitted by your employees), which may create legal liability or other risks for the organization.

Protecting Outbound Information

Content security is a means of protecting and managing valuable content. To that end, establish and enforce rules to prevent employees from:

- Overstating product or service capabilities

- E-mailing business secrets and other confidential information to outsiders, including competitors

- Stealing customer lists and other proprietary information as they leave your company to set up shop on their own

- Sending abusive, offensive, menacing, threatening, obscene, defamatory, or otherwise inappropriate messages

■ Illegally downloading pirated software and e-mailing it to friends, family, and coworkers

Content Filtering: Managing What Employees Say

Certain industries need (and may be legally required) to manage what employees say and do with e-mail. Brokerage firms, for example, must ensure that brokers do not make misrepresentations to potential investors. To keep the firm and its brokers out of trouble, some brokerages have supervisors review e-mail messages before they are sent to clients. The goal: to ensure compliance with SEC and NASD rules.

Some firms rely on automated search and filtering tools to do their internal auditing. Content filtering search tools allow management to monitor what brokers are saying via e-mail. If the technology spots target terms in a message's body or subject line, transmission is halted and the message is earmarked for manual review.

Consider, for example, this e-mail drafted by an investment broker.

> Teri and Missy,
>
> I hope you are both well. I have been thinking about you over the past couple years during the tumultuous stock market. It has been a rough time for all of us. In that regard, I want to tell you about a great investment opportunity. After all, we can all use a winner right now. I am strongly recommending Stink Bottom Rock Fishing Lures Co. Given the events of the past year, everyone is taking more time out to "smell the roses," making fishing more popular than ever. This stock is a guaranteed winner. BTW—please say hi to the kids for me.
>
> Lily Bugg

What's wrong with this e-mail? Could an automated filtering search tool help?

There are a number of potentially problematic words and

phrases that should perhaps be omitted from the message. Automated search tools could be used to root out suspect words and phrases, which then would be reviewed manually before transmission. In light of the firm's concern that brokers not overstate the attractiveness of investments, the filtering tool could have identified the following as questionable: "great," "winner," "strongly recommending," "guaranteed."

In addition, the firm likely could search for harassing, discriminatory, or other offensive content. In fact, technology can capture just about any content concern, including slang, inappropriate terms, profanity, flames (heated messages), or chilies (aggressive terms).

Is It Always Good to Filter Out the Bad?

In a word, yes. The easiest way to control e-risk is to control e-content. To that end, employees should be prohibited from using language that is in any way inappropriate or offensive—bad content.

But what happens when your filtering technology reveals that a number of employees are writing inappropriate messages that could potentially impact the organization and their own careers? For example, what if an audit uncovers the fact that twelve employees have shared "jokes" that disparage women, a clear violation of the organization's e-mail policy? Since management summarily fired an offending employee the last time this type of infraction occurred, the organization may have no choice but to fire all twelve violators or potentially face a claim that management selectively enforces its policy.

The bottom line is, if filtering reveals that employees are violating e-mail policy, you may have to take action, possibly decimating an otherwise good workforce in the process.

Combine Content Security Software with Policy and Education

To avoid a similar disaster, create a strategic e-risk management program based on the three Es of risk management: (1) *establish* written e-mail policy; (2) *educate* your workforce about e-risks and policy compliance; and (3) *enforce* your e-mail policy with policy-based content security software, such as Clearswift Corporation's MIMEsweeper and ENTERPRISEsuite product lines, which are designed to support your e-mail rules and risk management strategy.

Repudiation and Security

Scenario: A former vendor contacts you to inquire about an outstanding invoice. Your accounts receivable department researches the matter and notifies the vendor that their contract was terminated nearly four months earlier, pursuant to your organization's termination clause. The vendor replies that the contract was extended by your employee Rudy Rock. (Rock is the only employee with "signing" authority, a fact all employees and vendors have been advised of.) Your research reveals that an e-mail purportedly extending the contract was sent from Rock's e-mail account. Rock, however, denies sending the e-mail.

Facing a potential contract dispute, you have several problems to deal with: (1) Who sent the e-mail and why; (2) how was someone other than the authorized user able to access Rock's e-mail account; (3) how can you ensure that this never happens again; (4) will you be able to resolve the matter short of litigation; (5) was it reasonable for the vendor to rely on the e-mail; and (6) what security features could have prevented the situation from happening?

This scenario is more common and complicated than you might think. It seems reasonable that, if the two organizations have a history of doing business together via e-mail, one of the parties would make decisions based on e-mail that appears to come from a contact who can bind the organization. We know that the e-mail was received and the vendor relied on it to gear up to perform the contract again this year. It seems reasonable that the vendor should not be negatively impacted because Rock claims he did not send the e-mail extending the contract. After all, the vendor did nothing wrong. Or did it? What can you do to prevent someone from repudiating an agreement with your organization?

How to Protect Your Organization from Repudiation

1. Send and retain confirming e-mail messages.

2. Require authorizing purchase orders to be attached to e-mail.

3. Control active e-mail accounts.

4. For business transactions, require a secure electronic signature.

5. Develop a method of conducting business securely.

Recap and E-Action Plan

E-Mail Rule #29: Outbound E-Mail Is Critical to E-Mail Security

1. Be aware that inappropriate and offensive e-mail content (written and transmitted by your employees) may create legal liability or other risks for the organization.

2. Establish and enforce rules to prevent employees from writing and sending potentially damaging content.

3. Consider installing content filtering software to automate the process.

4. Combine e-mail policy with employee education and policy-based content security software designed to support your risk management goals.

5. Put rules and policies in place to protect the integrity of business transactions and avoid contract repudiation.

CHAPTER 30

E-Mail System Security

E-Mail Rule #30: Develop Policies and Procedures to Ensure That Your E-Mail System Is Secure

Secure E-Mail and Encryption Technology

E-mail sent in the "default" manner over the Internet is inherently insecure. The common analogy is that standard e-mail is like sending a "postcard written in pencil through the postal mail." A postcard, because anyone who sees the message along the way can freely read it, and pencil because the same person can easily alter the contents of the postcard.

Although the inherently insecure quality of e-mail may not be an issue for a certain class of administrative e-mail messages, it simply is not good enough for many e-mail messages used for business purposes. Do not be tempted to dismiss this security flaw under the guise of "everyone else does it," or "only 1 percent of our messages contain confidential information." This risk cannot be so easily dismissed.

Now is the time to get serious about your e-mail system. E-mail is a real business tool containing reams of information useful to competitors, adversaries in litigation, auditors, investigators, and criminal or malicious parties.

Perhaps you can confidently state that your employees never send proprietary information via e-mail. That's great. But do workers send more casual messages from which competitors or

malicious parties could glean information about product development or marketing plans? Could economic or environmental
protestors tap e-mail to learn the travel plans of your CEO and
high-profile board of directors? Does employee e-mail contain
details of internal squabbling that could devastate your stock
valuation and ruin executive careers if made public?

These are just a few of the many reasons why encrypting
e-mail messages may be critical for your organization.

Employ Encryption Technology Broadly

Few organizations employ e-mail encryption technology
broadly enough. Because few organizations view security issues
through a business lens, an investment in security technology is
often viewed as a drag on the bottom line, rather than as a
strategic investment. This attitude is changing over time, however, as more and more organizations fall victim to security
blunders.

In addition, it is difficult to change users' habits. Convincing
people to proactively apply encryption can be difficult. Another
problem is that the "digital credentials" required to send and
receive secure e-mail can be difficult and expensive to issue and
use. Finally, vendors have been slow to provide e-mail encryption products that meet all major business and technical
requirements. This is changing, though, as technology tools
grow in sophistication and demand for products increases.

Currently, the use of secure e-mail products is most common
in the government, legal, pharmaceutical, health care, insurance, and financial sectors—industries with clear business and
legal needs to protect information, while enhancing customer
service.

Benefits of Secure E-Mail

Secure e-mail should promote integrity, confidentiality/privacy,
authenticity, proof of receipt, and a shield from repudiation.

1. **Integrity.** This ensures that the contents of an e-mail message and its attachments have not been altered. Digital

signature technology, for example, creates a unique finger-print of an e-mail message before it is sent, then compares the original digital fingerprint to one that is generated by the recipient to determine if the message has changed. If the message has been altered, the new fingerprint created by the recipient will not be the same. This function is critical if you rely on e-mail to send and receive documents and information over which there could be some dispute, and you wish to prevent a party from claiming it agreed to a different version of a contract, for example.

2. **Confidentiality and privacy.** Designed to ensure that an e-mail message can be read only by its intended recipient, even if the message and its attachments are intercepted during transmission. This is critical in sectors such as health care, pharmaceuticals, financial services, insurance, and government, where there is a legal obligation to protect privacy. It is equally important for all businesses that use e-mail to send contracts and other sensitive information.

3. **Authenticity.** Businesses must be able to demonstrate who originated a message and who controlled it at various times during its lifecycle. This has been a central issue in discrimination cases, in which it was necessary to prove whether or not an individual actually sent a disputed e-mail. Authenticity is required for a variety of business purposes, such as holding contractors to promises made in e-mail, demonstrating that a response was made to a customer's concerns, or tracking down the originator of a libelous campaign to damage your organization's reputation.

4. **Proof of receipt.** As with postal mail, you sometimes must prove that a party received an e-mail message. In situations where timing is important, such as responding to a bid, providing a legal notice, or simply delivering a proposal or contract, having proof of delivery and receipt is key.

5. **Nonrepudiation.** In most business transactions, you need assurances that the other party will live up to his or her end of the bargain. In other words, you want to prevent parties from repudiating or disowning an e-mail message. You don't want the other party to claim not to have sent or

received an e-mail message or to dispute contractual terms. Nonrepudiation relies on secure e-mail qualities, including integrity, authenticity, and proof of receipt.

Understanding Technological Approaches

Your organization has a variety of options when it comes to selecting and implementing secure e-mail technology.

■ **Encryption.** Encryption is not an approach to secure e-mail in and of itself, but a technology common to most secure e-mail products. Encryption is a mathematical method for scrambling plain text and other digital information in such a way that it can be unscrambled and read only by someone who understands the secret method used to scramble it. The scrambling process is called "encryption," the unscrambling process "decryption," and the secret method a "cipher." A separate, secure channel is needed for exchanging the encryption/decryption keys.

Decryption keys are exchanged using secure lines, disks, or other techniques designed to protect them. A more advanced form of encryption uses a different key for encryption and decryption. This method has gained popularity on the Web in the form of Public Key Infrastructure (PKI), which simply provides the processes and technology for issuing and managing the keys and other digital credentials used to protect and ensure the integrity of digital information.

Encryption is used at many points in the secure e-mail process. Users might encrypt messages on their desktops before sending them. Administrators may apply encryption to stored e-mail to minimize the likelihood of unauthorized parties reading it. Secure online transactions with banks and online merchants involve encryption, too.

■ **Key-based e-mail security.** This approach to e-mail security uses various methods to create and distribute encryption/decryption keys and online credentials to parties who wish to communicate via secure e-mail. Several PKI vendors issue keys and credentials, so employees in an organization can encrypt and sign e-mail. Message integrity is ensured, as messages can be decrypted only by intended recipients and cannot be changed by unauthorized parties. Authenticity is promoted when employees' online credentials are used to connect messages with their authors. Nonrepudiation is advanced because the policies, practices, and technology used typically are defined in a manner that adds to overall system trustworthiness.

A drawback to this model is the complexity and expense of issuing and managing keys and credentials. There are, however, simplified methods in which keys are managed at the server level, and content is "wrapped" in Java code and delivered as a basic e-mail attachment to be opened by any Web browser without the need for a key on the desktop.

■ **Web-based methods.** The Web mailbox approach is a secure e-mail model providing Web-based e-mail service. The user takes no action to encrypt or decrypt messages on the desktop; instead, e-mail messages are automatically encrypted and decrypted using the Web browser's built-in Secure Sockets Layer (SSL). Communication is limited to subscribers.

The Web courier method employs a standard Web browser and a secure Web site that "delivers" and "picks up" secure messages. In this scenario, a sender uploads an e-mail message and attachment to a secure Web site, which automatically generates an unsecured e-mail informing the recipient that a "package" is awaiting pickup at the specified URL. Using a preassigned password, the recipient logs in and retrieves the message, which is then deleted from the server.

While Web-based methods may meet the needs of many organizations, a primary drawback is that they are not integrated with the e-mail system used to send and receive the majority of messages. Switching back and forth is cumbersome for users, and another location and information/records channel requires management.

■ **Secure e-mail gateways.** This emerging method uses encryption software that resides not on each user's computer, but on a server that sits between the internal network and the Internet or is integrated as part of an enterprise e-mail server. Encryption software encrypts and decrypts e-mail messages in real time as they move into and out of the organization. Such systems are attractive to many organizations because they do not require software on the desktop, and encryption and other security controls can be applied automatically based on content and content policies at the server. These solutions also bring control in-house, without relying on an outsourced firm.

Recap and E-Action Plan

E-Mail Rule #30: Develop Policies and Procedures to Ensure That Your E-Mail System Is Secure

Deciding which secure e-mail product or technology is right for you depends on a number of variables:

1. **Organization size.** Larger operations have larger e-mail volumes that call for enterprise solutions.

2. **Corporate culture.** Secure e-mail technology requires a change in the way your organization thinks about e-mail. It also requires a significant investment in technology, training, and policy development.

3. **Comfort with outsourcing.** Many Web-based products are designed and delivered as a service by relatively new companies. If you are comfortable with this type of relationship, a service like this can be an important tool in your e-mail management arsenal, without a large initial outlay of capital. Remember, however, that there are always legal and business issues to consider when outsourcing critical business functions to third parties. Your service provider's failure to adequately protect its facilities, for example, will expose your organization to substantial risks.

4. **Necessary features.** Any decision about secure e-mail products should be driven by legal and business issues, as well as security needs.

CHAPTER 31

Spam

E-Mail Rule #31: Address the Sending, Forwarding, and Receiving of Spam in Your E-Mail Policy

The electronic equivalent of junk mail, spam is unsolicited e-mail that is neither wanted nor needed by the hapless recipient. IDC research reveals that 1.5 billion spam mailings hit corporate inboxes in 2001, representing about 20 percent of all business e-mail in the United States.[1]

According to one survey, the number of monthly spam attacks grew from 880,000 to nearly 5 million in the 18 months between January 2001 and June 2002. The survey's breakdown of top spam categories: general goods and services 27 percent; financial opportunities 20 percent; computer-related material 13 percent; adult information/pornography 8 percent; frauds and scams 6 percent.[2]

Thanks to the post–September 11, 2001, anthrax scare, we're seeing more spam than ever. Both the Gartner Group and IDC report a 16-fold increase in spam over the past two years.[3]

All that spam is taking quite a financial toll, inflicting an annual cost of 10 billion euros, US$8.7 billion, on Internet users.[4] Spam is a nightmare for IT managers. As IDC and Clearswift report, about 39 percent of e-mail is spam. In a typical

1,000-employee organization, approximately 2.1 million spam messages are received and circulated every year. The cost of dealing with spam on a network that size is about $6.5 million.[5] That is a big waste of assets—human, computer, and financial.

What Makes E-Mail So Appealing to Direct Marketers?

Direct marketers who once relied on snail mail to solicit business are increasingly turning to e-mail spam. Unfortunately for recipients, e-mail offers direct marketers a number of advantages over snail mail:

■ Spam's 3 to 5 percent response rate tops the 1 to 2 percent response rate of direct marketing snail mail.

■ Mass e-mail campaigns are cheap—no postage, no paper, no printing costs.

■ Spammers can send hundreds of thousands of unsolicited messages simply by clicking "send."

Direct marketers are not the only spammers in cyberspace. According to the Gartner Group, 25 percent of all e-mail is either trash spam promoting fraudulent schemes or e-junk including chain letters, urban legends, and hoaxes.[6]

Spam Creates Workplace Liabilities

More than a nuisance, spam carries a hefty price tag. Among spam's common and potentially costly risks:

1. **Legal liability.** Take the case of the U.S. energy company that was bombarded by the most offensive type of spam imaginable, child pornography, for two years. Management did nothing to stop the flow of X-rated spam until fed-up employees took matters into their own hands and visited the FBI. Fearful that the employees would file suit on the grounds of a hostile work environment or that the FBI would launch an investigation, the CEO finally ordered

the installation of antispam software and the development of a written e-mail policy addressing the sending, receiving, and forwarding of spam.

2. **Displacement of business e-mail.** When an employee of Lockheed Martin spammed 60,000 coworkers, including a request for an electronic receipt, the defense contractor's legitimate e-mail system crashed. It took a Microsoft rescue squad six hours to get the company's e-mail system up and running again.[7]

3. **Lost productivity.** E-mail has replaced the water cooler as the number-one time-waster in offices. According to one recent survey, nearly 30 percent of e-mail users receive jokes and chain letters daily. Fully 70 percent of employees admit sending junk e-mail.[8]

Consider the impact on network productivity, too. It's estimated that 2 to 10 percent of corporations' inbound Internet e-mail is spam, with that number expected to grow to 10 to 20 percent over the next five years. Add these additional messages to an organization's network infrastructure, and the result is a costly one, including hardware for storing and handling messages and bandwidth for processing.[9]

Not surprisingly, bandwidth problems rank number four among e-mail filter user concerns, according to a 2001 IDC survey. Most users buy e-mail filters and related products in response to concerns over security, legal liability, employee productivity, and network bandwidth.[10]

What's the Solution?

The spam problem is not easily solved. Senders of spam always seem to find clever new ways to keep their e-mail from being blocked. Blocking spam with technology is challenging, because one organization's spam is another company's legitimate content. The best solution is a three-pronged approach: (1) establish a content security policy that addresses spam as a threat; (2) educate employees about spam and e-mail policy compliance; and (3) implement appropriate technology to block spam at the gateway, eliminating the need for desktop management of unsolicited e-mail.

Tell Employees What to Look For

To enhance your employee education efforts, instruct employees to avoid spammers' favorite tricks.[11]

1. **Phony subject line.** Knowing security is looking for specific headers, spammers will intentionally misspell words ("you are this months priz winer" or "loose 30 pounds in 7 days."

2. **Numeric address formats.** Spam often uses addresses with numeric versions to avoid blocking based on previous spam e-mail recognition. For example, the sender's address might read: philr1210@mail.spike; philr1211@mail.spike; philr1212@mail.spike.

3. **Celebrity subject headers.** Message headers that mention celebrities typically are spam.

4. **Dictionary spam.** If a message's "To" field is crowded with e-mail addresses containing names similar to yours, you've been dictionary spammed. The spammer sends out multiple variations of e-mail addresses and domains to see what hits.

5. **Spurious content.** If an e-mail says you can make a million dollars working from home, while enlarging your breasts and losing 10 inches from your hips and waist, it's spam.

6. **Bogus unsubscribe links.** Legitimate marketers honor unsubscribe requests. Spammers use them to verify your address and send more spam. Never reply to the unsubscribe option unless you want to respond to the spammer's sales pitch.

7. **Phony return address.** Most bulk e-mailers can generate random false return addresses. Don't be surprised if they use your e-mail address, too.

8. **Forged headers:** Check the headers of incoming e-mail. Spammers falsify routing headers, the trail left by mail servers as e-mail passes, to hide their location.

9. **Common spam categories.** If these words or subject categories appear on the subject line, it's probably spam: Pornography, Money Making, Direct Products, Become a Spammer, Gambling/Sweepstakes, Health Cures/Weight Loss.

What to Look for in Antispam Software

Antispam products should work in conjunction with your e-mail policy and offer various tools to help weed out annoying e-mail. Because spam is not universally defined, antispam tools should be flexible, allowing your organization to customize its approach.

It is important that your organization be empowered to block as much unwanted e-mail as possible.

Buyer beware. Many antispam products claim that they can stop 99 percent of unwanted e-mail. That sometimes indicates a high number of false positives. Make sure that your software doesn't take up so much administrative time unblocking legitimate e-mails that the return on investment is lost.

Two Quick Spam-Busting Techniques

1. **Don't feel obligated to read and respond to every message.** Fully 96 percent of executives read and respond to their own e-mail, according to an ePolicy Institute/International Association of Administrative Professionals (IAAP) survey. No wonder it takes execs half the day to sort and send messages. Before opening mail, scan the subject line and delete obvious spam.

2. **Empower an electronic gatekeeper.** Armed with a valid e-mail address, spammers can slip past administrative assistants and communicate directly with decision-makers. While nearly all executives are reading and replying to at least some of their own e-mail, 26 percent assign their administrative professionals the task of screening incoming e-mail, and 29 percent authorize a gatekeeper to delete messages. Keep your mailbox spam free by making your assistant your electronic gatekeeper.[12]

Don't Bet Your Future on Antispam Legislation

The move to legally outlaw spam is gaining ground. Among the many antispam laws in the works is the Controlling the Assault of Non-Solicited Pornography and Marketing Act of 2001 (CAN SPAM Act), which may become U.S. federal law in the near future. In addition, twenty states have imposed various antispam laws, some of which require genuine return e-mail addresses and opt-out options.

In May 2002, the European Parliament voted to ban spam. Under the directive, which should be in place in 2003, people must opt in, or ask to receive, commercial e-mail.

That said, do not expect legislators to fight your spam battle for you. Most spam either originates or is routed from foreign countries. The impact of U.S. legislation on foreign spammers may be minimal, at best.

At the end of the day, spam is an organizational problem that requires an organizational solution based on establishing policy, educating employees, and enforcing compliance.

Recap and E-Action Plan

E-Mail Rule #31: Address the Sending, Forwarding, and Receiving of Spam in Your E-Mail Policy

1. Spam wastes financial, human, and computer assets.

2. Establish a content security policy that addresses e-mail spam as a threat.

3. Educate employees about spam and e-mail policy compliance.

4. Implement technology to block spam at the gateway and eliminate the need for desktop management of unsolicited e-mail.

PART SIX

Mixed Messages: Managing Alternative Communications Technologies

CHAPTER 32

Instant Messaging
E-Mail Rule #32: Retain and Manage Business Records Created by Alternative Communications Technologies

Although e-mail is a powerful tool, enabling fast and inexpensive global transmission of text and other forms of data, it has an inherent flaw: It's not instant. For the more than 100 million people worldwide who use Instant Messaging (IM),[1] e-mail simply isn't fast enough.

IM appeals to users looking for a more chatty way of communicating remotely. That's appropriate, given that IM lends itself to the ongoing exchange of short sentences. Chat, in other words. Businesses appreciate IM's impact on internal and external communications, as questions may be asked and feedback provided in real time.

The popularity of IM is soaring. It is estimated that by 2005, it will be used more often worldwide than e-mail.[2] With 42 percent of U.S. companies already using or planning to use IM,[3] business probably will account for half the estimated 530 million IM users projected to be online by 2006.[4]

Although its main function is chat, IM offers a range of features, including:

▓ Direct transfer of data files.

▓ Direct sending and receiving of messages to and from cell phones, pagers, telephones, and fax machines.

■ Voice-over-IP, combining a computer with IM software for voice communication. You use your computer just like a telephone.

■ Sending and receiving e-mail messages.

■ Web conferencing, application sharing, and remote control of another computer.

■ Subscriptions to content channels providing news updates, stock information, sports, weather, and other information.

■ Monitoring when other parties are signed in to the IM system.

IM Challenges for Business Users

According to Gartner Group, there were 18.5 million corporate IM users in 2001, with 70 percent of U.S. companies expected to use the technology by 2003.[5] Employers considering IM should bear in mind that the technology was originally intended for home use. There are, therefore, concerns for business users:

1. **Security.** IM lacks built-in protections against destructive payloads, such as Trojan horses and viruses. Unless IM messages are identified and controlled by firewalls or other network security devices, they may open your network to attack.

2. **Administration.** IM provides limited tools for its management and data or record control.

3. **Archiving.** Tools for capturing and archiving IM communications generally are not provided with IM software. This void has allowed companies like Legato Systems, Inc., and others to develop IM storage and retention solutions.

Developing and Applying IM Business Rules

Like other communication technology used for business, IM creates information that should be managed as business records according to written business rules. Your greatest challenge will be giving employees cutting-edge, productivity-enhancing tools, while keeping your organization out of harm's way.

First, decide if you even want to permit IM use. That said, understand that the technology is probably being used now without your knowledge or approval. If employees are using IM to communicate with friends and family, you must act. Company equipment, networks, and time are being used, creating potential business and legal problems. On the legal side, unsupervised use of IM can lead to inappropriate content and potential liability. Without proper management of information and business records, corporate IM users put the organization at risk.

Productivity is an issue, too. IM users tend to chat often. Use written policy to spell out clearly that the company provides IM to augment business productivity, not as a diversion from work.

Three Different Approaches to Workplace IM Use

1. **Ban IM altogether.** You may decide the risks of IM outweigh its benefits. If so, take steps to prevent rogue use:
   a. Forbid IM use in employee acceptable-use policies.
   b. Do not install IM technology on employee computers.
   c. Configure firewalls and networks to block IM messages.
   d. Limit the use of communications devices that allow IM at work.

2. **Allow personal IM use.** Not the recommended approach, your organization may opt to allow employees to use IM for personal communication, in exchange for working longer hours or some other concession to management. If you choose this approach, be sure to provide guidance on how much personal IM time is allowed, and during what times of the day (before and after regular working hours, during breaks, etc.). Understand, however, that once you open the door to a little personal use, your employees will likely kick it wide open. Generally it's better to leave this door closed—and locked.

3. **Legitimize and enable work use.** If you decide IM technology will enhance interoffice communication, customer service, and communication with remote employees, be sure to develop business rules that outline acceptable uses. You also will need to invest in the infrastructure and tools necessary to manage IM as a business asset. Off-the-shelf consumer-oriented IM products generally don't provide the level of control and security needed by business.

Recap and E-Action Plan

E-Mail Rule #32: Retain and Manage Business Records Created by Alternative Communications Technologies

1. **Acceptable use.** Specify what type of use is acceptable, and what is not. For example, consider IM when a record of the communication will not be needed or when a longer, more detailed e-mail message is not required. Make it clear that IM communication with friends and family is not acceptable.

2. **Standardization.** Adopt and support one IM tool. Make it clear that other IM brands are not allowed. This will make the administration and retention of IM messages easier. It will also allow you to control how IM is used by preventing messages written on unrecognized tools from leaving your network.

3. **Features.** IM can be used for purposes beyond text messaging, including sharing digital media files and controlling remote computers. You may wish to limit IM use to chat only, or you could apply policies and administrative controls that allow only word processing documents to be transferred via IM.

4. **Security.** Unless IM is legitimized with appropriate business rules, enterprise-grade tools, and IT involvement, security risks loom. Inform IT managers if IM is to be allowed, so they can open and manage the network ports through which IM travels.

    If not managed according to well-defined rules, open

ports can be used by malicious hackers to damage corporate networks. Some IM users have been tricked into downloading files by parties posing as system administrators or ISP billing agents. In one case, a downloaded virus gained remote control of the user's computer, exposing confidential data, installing malicious software, and altering and deleting files.[6]

5. **Retention.** Just like e-mail, IM used for business purposes generates information with potential business and legal significance. Your organization must apply rules for identifying, retaining, and managing information and business records. Some regulators, such as the National Association of Securities Dealers (NASD), require IM messages to be managed with the same care as e-mail messages. Since retention rules depend on the technological ability to retain messages, you will need to provide retention functionality for users.

6. Train employees to retain and classify required IM exchanges. If, for example, your IM system and rules allow external IM communication to customers, then the retention of all outbound and inbound IM messages may be appropriate. As with e-mail, employees should be trained to recognize and retain exchanges that have business and legal significance, and to discard those that do not.

CHAPTER 33

Other Communications Technologies
E-Mail Rule #33: Establish E-Rules and Training for Alternative Technologies

Short Messaging Service (SMS) and mobile e-mail devices such as the BlackBerry™ are gaining prominence as business tools. With 1 billion SMS messages sent daily in the United States and Canada,[1] and tens of thousands of organizations subscribing to wireless e-mail services,[2] it's likely that someone in your organization is already using one of these technologies for business purposes. Be sure you have e-rules and training in place to cover their use.

SMS

With SMS being long popular in Europe and Asia, some 250 billion SMS messages were sent worldwide in 2001.[3] North America is catching up quickly, with use of SMS, or mobile phone originated text messages, up some 400 percent in 2002.[4] In the United States, mobile phones and networks are being updated to enable SMS.[5]

SMS technology allows owners of digital mobile phones to send and receive short text messages to and from other mobile phones. These "disposable" SMS messages are rarely retained by their senders or recipients, thanks to the nature of the service and the relatively small storage capacity of mobile phones.

SMS, like Instant Messaging, appeals to business because of its instantaneous nature: Messages are "pushed" to the recipient's phone immediately. SMS also can be used to broadcast the same message to multiple recipients, which is a useful feature for workgroups and teams. Many users like the fact that SMS limits messages to few characters, encouraging brevity in business communication.

Mobile E-Mail

The various ways to send and receive e-mail from wireless devices include:

* Laptops with wireless capabilities

* Mobile phones

* Wireless Personal Digital Assistants (PDAs) and handhelds

* E-mail-specific devices, such as the BlackBerry, designed for business use

Communications from these devices are managed like any other e-mail messages.

An added "benefit" to mobile e-mail devices: They provide one more source of copies, drafts, and transmitted messages for discovery. In light of the sensitive information sometimes contained in e-mail, mobile wireless should be used only within the context of an enterprise's wireless information security strategy.

Applying Business Rules to SMS

While the basic management and control guidelines suggested for IM in the previous chapter apply to SMS, be aware that SMS may be the more difficult technology to control and manage. Unless enterprise-grade tools are used to implement SMS, the retention of business content is difficult. The limited memory and output options of a mobile phone make retention on the device difficult, and the reliance on outside network providers makes central retention a challenge. In short, the technology is not yet mainstream for use as a real business tool.

In spite of the inability to store messages electronically, be sure to develop policy and rules governing how employees handle SMS messages requiring retention. You might, for example, require recipients to transcribe messages onto paper, complete with metadata including the date, time, and sender.

For maximum risk management, either don't purchase SMS service or have your provider disable it from company-provided mobile phones.

Other Centralized Forums

Instant Messaging is not the only way to chat online or hold cyber-discussions. Where point-to-point technology allows IM/SMS-enabled computers and devices to communicate directly with one another, centralized technology uses a central server, Web service, or virtual room for chatting and discussion.

Centralization (to the extent you control the forum) makes the identification, retention, and management of important business content and records much easier than IM. However, centralized message boards, which may encourage frank and informal discussion without the benefit of rules and controls, can be a significant source of liability and risk.

Some of the most common types of centralized online chat and discussion forums are detailed below. (See also discussion about LISTSERV® in Chapter 9.)

Proprietary Discussion Boards

Bundled within some e-mail software is a discussion board feature that allows employees to set up their own in-house discussion area. Useful for sharing business ideas, these proprietary chat rooms tend to be casual and free-flowing. Compounding the problem, management may not know the staff has established a discussion board. Making matters worse, if e-mail is being backed up, the discussion databases probably are being backed up as well. Any relevant information, including ultra-casual discussion board chat, is potentially discoverable. Business rules dealing with discussion board use and message retention must be developed before employees create and use chat areas.

Newsgroups

Newsgroups provide forums for online discussion via the posting and viewing of text-based messages to topic-based news groups. Posting and viewing can be done through a Web browser or dedicated "news reader" e-mail software.

While newsgroups share similarities with e-mail, the primary difference is that "sent" messages are posted to the newsgroup, where any subscriber can read them.

Tens of thousands of public newsgroups on just about every imaginable topic exist. Businesses can create private newsgroups on their own servers, which only designated subscribers can access. Software vendors, for example, often use this technique to provide customer support forums for their products.

Web-Based Message Boards

Web-based message boards and discussion areas are similar to newsgroups, in that subscribers post and read messages. The primary difference is that all posting and reading are done through a Web browser instead of newsreader software. Like newsgroups, message boards often are used externally by organizations for customer relations, internally for work-related discussions. Related technology enables real-time discussion on the message boards.

In terms of information management, message boards offer unique challenges. Where newsgroups create individual stand-alone messages and can be captured and managed as such, message board "comments" generate a stream of information more akin to Web browsing data.

Recap and E-Action Plan

E-Mail Rule #33: Establish E-Rules and Training for Alternative Technologies

1. **Public access.** Decide whether your employees should have access to public newsgroups and message boards. These forums, particularly public newsgroups, may contain offen-

sive or illegal content that could create legal issues for your organization if downloaded by an employee. On the up-side, industry forums can help employees keep abreast of professional developments.

2. **Filtering.** If you decide to outlaw public newsgroup partici-pation, find out if your Internet provider or IT administra-tor can block the technology.

3. **Develop rules for the use of public forums.**
   a. Clarify what type of newsgroups, message boards, and forums employees may subscribe to. Consider limiting subscriptions to those related to your industry or em-ployees' professional development.
   b. Consider restricting employees to "read only" status. They can read but not post. By prohibiting posting, you eliminate the liability associated with employees making inappropriate comments or embarrassing admissions about the company in a public forum.

      If you allow employees to post, provide guidelines on content. As with e-mail guidelines, address the use of company message signatures and other information that identifies an employee of your organization as the post-ing's author. Many organizations add disclaimers to the body of every e-mail sent by an employee. Statements such as "the opinions expressed in this e-mail are the author's only" are designed to protect the organization from liability caused by an employee's e-mail message. Such legends should be considered when employees use company e-mail to post to public newsgroups and other message boards.
   c. Suggest how much time employees may spend contrib-uting to public forums.
   d. Some newsgroups and message boards are moderated by an individual who reviews each message before post-ing to determine if it adheres to group rules. Moderated public groups tend to post content that is less problem-atic than freewheeling groups. This is a consideration when developing business rules related to public forums.

4. **Develop rules for in-house forums.**
   a. Make it clear that e-mail content guidelines apply equally to forum postings.

b. Apply retention rules. If retention in electronic form is not possible, develop rules for paper-based retention. Some content, such as unique and new ideas and observations, is unlikely to be considered a record requiring retention and therefore should not be retained. In any event, rules can help employees do the right thing.

c. Consider retention location. Minimize your storage burden by enacting policies that prevent users from retaining local copies of information. Retain and provide a centrally accessible archive when the nature and value of the content dictates its use.

d. Encourage employees to keep postings on topic and follow other guidelines or rules regarding type of content, professionalism, frequency of posting, and use of attachments. Every moderated newsgroup (and many that are nonmoderated) publishes posting rules, a useful starting point for your organization.

CHAPTER 34

Peer-to-Peer File Networking Technology

E-Mail Rule #34: Combine Employee Rules with Network Administration Techniques to Limit Risks

Peer-to-peer (P2P) enables one computer to locate another on a network and communicate directly with it. The ability to communicate directly, rather than through a centralized server managed by the organization, makes P2P technology both a boon and a threat to your organization.

Networking 101

The Web and other common networking architectures are based on the concepts of server and client. The server acts as a central repository of the data to be distributed or published. A server can be as simple as a desktop computer, although it often has more disk space, a faster network connection, and software that controls which clients access what content. The client is another computer connected to the network.

A Web server contains text and code for Web pages and related images, sound files, etc. When you connect to a Web site, your computer is acting as a client. Your Web browser sends a request to the Web server, which responds by allowing your computer to download and view a Web page.

Part of the magic of the Web is that your client computer is able to find and communicate with public Web servers all over the planet. This is accomplished through a global "telephone directory" that assigns a unique number to each computer on the Internet, then automatically connects clients and servers wishing to talk.

This "phone book," however, contains only the "numbers" of servers. So, if two clients want to talk to each other, there is no easy way for them to find each other. This is where P2P networking comes in. It allows two clients who are equal members of a network, or peers, to act as clients and servers. In this model, any computer on the network can act as a server and publish information, and any computer can act as a client and request information for download. P2P technology also provides its own global phone directory with the unique numbers of the network's peer computers.

P2P Technology

Every network provides some sort of directory for computers to find and talk with each other. While the most common methods on the Internet are standardized and nonproprietary, P2P standards are largely emerging and proprietary. P2P's most common approaches are the centralized directory and the distributed directory.

The centralized directory relies on a server that hosts the names and numbers of all of the computers in the network. This is the model that Napster, the music file sharing network, employed. Once you joined the Napster network, the central server would collect your computer's Internet address and the list of files you were sharing and store it in a central directory. Other Napster users could then search the central directory for a desired file, connect to your computer, and download files.

The distributed directory uses a similar method, but there is no centralized directory. Instead, information about your computer and shared files is stored on several other computers that are equal members of the network. In fact, your own computer can be used to store the same information about other computers. The directory information from each of these "node" computers is used for locating other computers and conducting searches.

P2P relies on proprietary software residing on peer computers. The software is used for sending and receiving P2P messages necessary to locate other computers. It's also used for searching computers for files. In addition, the software may enable users to designate which area of the hard drive they wish to share with other users.

P2P Threats

In a 2002 e-mail message to all employees, a Microsoft executive expressed concerns about P2P: "Running such programs on company PCs or through company servers substantially increases the risk that our network could be hacked, that viruses could be introduced into our network, and that internal corporate documents could inadvertently be shared with others outside the company."[1]

Think carefully before allowing employees to tap into consumer-oriented P2P file-trading networks. At this time, the risks may outweigh the rewards. If you decide to allow P2P use, then be sure to combine basic employee rules with network administration techniques to limit your exposure as much as possible. Some of the liabilities and risks P2P can trigger follow.

Risk 1: Bandwidth Use

P2P file trading networks offer one of the most convenient ways to distribute large digital files. Inherent to P2P, then, is heavy bandwidth use. Unless files are being transmitted for legitimate business purposes, valuable bandwidth and hard drive space are being wasted on frivolous content.

Risk 2: Security

Because employee use of P2P can open a direct pipeline from hackers into your enterprise, you need to address network security before allowing the technology.

File trading works by exposing folders and directories to other network users, effectively opening up your computer system to the world. Although desktop software is designed to prevent other users from accessing areas beyond those designated, it is possible to defeat this protection unless proper management and security controls are in place.

It's also relatively easy for a user to disguise a Trojan horse, virus, or other malicious code as another file type, in order to trick users into downloading it directly to their hard drives. The result may be extensive damage to your organization's computer system.

Risk 3: Legal and Copyright Concerns

Record labels, film studios, software vendors, and other copyright holders have been aggressive in prosecuting copyright infringement perpetrated through P2P. Allowing your employees to trade copyright-protected files through the organization's equipment and networks may subject your organization to legal problems and other risks.

Recap and E-Action Plan

E-Mail Rule #34: Combine Employee Rules with Network Administration Techniques to Limit Risks

1. The ability for computers to communicate directly with one another makes P2P technology a communications boon as well as a legal threat.

2. Currently, the risks of consumer-oriented P2P use outweigh the rewards.

3. Limit risks by combining rules with employee training and network administration technology.

CHAPTER 35

E-Mail Variations
E-Mail Rule #35: Apply E-Mail Rules to Nontraditional Use and Technologies

There are various nontraditional ways to send and receive e-mail or to use e-mail and other communications technologies for nontraditional purposes. Not surprisingly, each comes with its own set of business and legal considerations.

Direct E-Mail

Favored by marketers who engage in mass e-mailings, direct e-mail bypasses the corporate or ISP e-mail server and sends messages directly to the recipient's e-mail server. Used to reduce the burden on e-mail servers and speed the sending of newsletters and similar material, direct e-mail also could be used to circumvent the capture and retention of employee e-mail. Consider establishing a rule to prevent or limit its use.

Web Mail

With Web-based mail (Microsoft's Hotmail® service and Yahoo!®), e-mail is sent and received via a Web browser, rather than dedicated e-mail software. Web-based e-mail accounts enable employees to send and receive e-mail messages that may sidestep the organization's e-mail infrastructure. Personal accounts may be used to bring inappropriate content into your organization and onto your company-owned computers. Employees also may use their personal accounts to send confidential or proprietary information to outsiders. Be sure to address the use of personal Web mail in your written rules and policies.

Recap and E-Action Plan

E-Mail Rule #35: Apply E-Mail Rules to Nontraditional Use and Technologies

1. Employees can use Web gateways, direct e-mail, and Web mail to circumvent your organization's rules, filters, and retention policies.

2. Address the use, misuse, and abuse of nontraditional e-mail technologies in your written e-mail policies.

3. Keep content clean, confidential information secure, and legal liabilities in check by giving employees rules for e-mail use—traditional e-mail and all its variations.

PART SEVEN
Employee Education

CHAPTER 36

Training Is Key to E-Risk Management Success
E-Mail Rule #36: Train, Train, Train . . . Then Train Some More

The courts and regulators appreciate and tend to respond favorably to consistently applied policy and training. Adopt the e-mail rules outlined in this book, draft a comprehensive e-mail policy, and institute a program of employee education, and you may find your workforce more compliant and the courts more accepting of the fact that you have made a reasonable effort to keep your organization free of discriminatory, harassing, hostile, or otherwise objectionable behavior.

In other words, written e-mail rules and policies coupled with an effective employee education program may help your organization defend workplace lawsuits and other e-risks.

Base Training on Your Organization's E-Mail Rules

To be an effective part of your e-risk management program, employee education should work hand in glove with your written e-mail rules and policies. The best training is ongoing and comprehensive. Depending on your organization's risks, policies, rules, and resources, employee training might address:

■ **E-mail risks and liabilities** facing the organization and individual employees.

■ **E-mail content.** What is, and is not, acceptable and appropriate.

■ **E-mail ownership and privacy.** What are your organization's responsibilities and your employees' rights?

■ **E-mail business records.** What must be retained, why, when, and how.

■ **E-mail retention and deletion.** Understanding the organization's rules and the individual employee's role.

■ **Industry and governmental regulations.** Toeing the line and staying in business.

■ **E-mail as legal evidence.** Complying with discovery processes and destruction prohibitions.

■ **Security breaches and cybertheft.** Keeping confidential information safe and secure.

■ **Netiquette.** Keeping online employees in-line.

■ **LISTSERVs,** road warriors, e-mail variations, and alternative communication technologies.

■ **Security and spam.** Maintaining a safe and secure working environment.

If that sounds like a lot of ground to cover, you're right. The topics that should be addressed in an ongoing employee education program are as far-reaching as the risks you face every time an employee accesses your e-mail system.

First, Rally the Support of Managers[1]

You can devote enormous amounts of time and talent to researching, planning, and writing your organization's e-mail rules and policies, only to see your guidelines fail if you don't devote an equal amount of attention to implementation and enforcement. Without an ongoing commitment to comprehensive employee education, you really cannot expect your employees to comply or your e-risk management program to succeed.

Effective education begins with your managers and supervisors. Before communicating your new e-mail rules and policies to employees, be sure that your managers, supervisors, and executives are on board as policy advocates and enforcers.

To that end, it is essential that you conduct training for the executive and management ranks prior to employee training. Give your management team ample time to ask questions and express concerns they may not be comfortable communicating in front of employees. Do not proceed with employee training until you are certain that all executives, managers, and supervisors are 100 percent behind the organization's e-risk management goals and are committed to enforcing your e-mail rules and policies.

If you sense resistance among some executives and managers, spend a little extra time discussing their concerns. Workplace e-risks, e-mail rules, and e-mail policies are relatively new concepts. Do not expect everyone to immediately grasp the dangers inherent in e-communications or the importance of complying with rules and policies.

For best results, structure e-mail policy training as an ongoing educational program, not a one-time session.

In the Battle Against E-Risks, Managers Form the Front Line of Defense

The success of your e-risk management program depends largely on management's willingness to embrace the organization's new e-mail rules and policies and share that enthusiasm with their troops. Your training goals for senior staff differ from employee training goals. Not only do you want executives, managers, and supervisors to comply with your new e-mail rules and policies, but you also want them to enforce the e-risk program among the employees they oversee.

Fill managers in on the risks inherent in, and the costs associated with, inappropriate e-mail use. Managers who are themselves responsible for departmental hiring, training, and budgeting will appreciate the financial loss and productivity drain e-risks represent.

Support management education by developing a special e-leadership training manual. Include in that manual a recap of your organization's e-risks. Add to your e-leadership training manual netiquette guidelines for managers. To ensure that they apply the rules consistently, consider providing managers with a breakdown, by violation, of the disciplinary action employees will face if they fail to comply with the organization's e-mail rules and policies.

Train Your Trainers

Once your organization's e-mail rules and policies are introduced to employees, you will want to rely on your managers, along with your legal, HR, and IT departments, to conduct ongoing employee education to enforce e-mail policy compliance. A few training tips to share with managers who may or may not be experienced trainers:

1. Understand that most employees are concerned about themselves first, the organization second. When training employees, focus less on organizational e-risks, and more on the penalties individual employees will face for noncompliance. Employees will look to their managers for clear direction on what they need to do and what they should avoid doing in order to comply with e-mail rules and e-mail policies—and hold onto their jobs.

2. Treat employees fairly and with respect. Assure workers that they will not be disciplined for computer system abuses that occurred prior to the development of the organization's e-mail rules and e-mail policies. Make it clear, however, that with new rules and policies now in place, employees will face disciplinary action, up to and including termination, for e-mail policy violations.

3. Enforce the organization's e-mail rules and policies consistently. Make an example out of one e-mail policy violator today, and you may avoid terminating dozens (or hundreds) of electronic rule-breakers tomorrow. Need convincing? The courts appreciate consistency. Your ability to walk into court and demonstrate a clear pattern of consistently enforcing written rules and policies may serve as a powerful weapon in your defense arsenal.

Recap and E-Action Plan

E-Mail Rule #36: Train, Train, Train . . . Then Train Some More

1. The courts and regulators appreciate—and tend to respond favorably to—policy and training consistently applied.

2. Written e-mail rules and policies coupled with an effective employee education program may help your organization deflect workplace lawsuits and other e-risks.

3. Base training on your organization's e-mail rules.

4. Start by educating executives, managers, and supervisors—the front lines of e-risk management success.

CHAPTER 37

Instilling a Sense of Ownership in Employees
E-Mail Rule #37: Employee Compliance Is Key to E-Risk Management Success

To be successful, your organization's e-mail rules and policies must be embraced by your employees.[1] It is not enough to establish a rule, draft a policy, review it once with employees, and then store it on a shelf in the HR director's office. That type of passive approach tells employees that the organization does not take its own policies seriously. So why should employees comply with them?

Effective e-risk management depends in part on your success at creating in workers and managers a true sense of e-mail policy ownership. If employees believe the organization's e-mail rules and policies have been designed to create a better working environment while ensuring a safe and secure future for the organization and the individual, they are more likely to support e-mail rules and policies.

Your employees do, after all, have the right to work in an environment free from harassment, discrimination, and hostility of any kind. And your comprehensive e-mail rules and e-mail policies are designed to accomplish just that. Training will play a valuable role in communicating to employees that the organization's e-risk management program exists as much for the benefit of the individual employee as for the organization as a whole.

Tips for Training Employees

Because of the relative newness of e-risks and e-rules, the most effective way to notify employees of your e-mail policies is in person. Depending on the size of your organization, you may want to hold a single group meeting for all employees. Larger organizations may opt for a series of smaller meetings, held over a period of one or two days. Training tips to help rally employee support and compliance include:

1. Show employees you mean business by having a senior company official (the more senior the better) introduce the organization's e-mail rules and e-mail policies to employees.

2. If a senior executive wants to conduct the entire training program, great. If not, assign in-house experts from various departments the roles of e-mail policy trainers. Your in-house legal counsel, human resources director, and chief information officer could each be called on to discuss the organization's electronic liabilities and review newly minted e-mail rules and policies.

3. Begin training with a recap of the liabilities and risks facing the organization, from lawsuits and lost productivity, to security breaches and spam, to viruses and hacker attacks. Attach dollar figures to risks whenever possible. And be sure to incorporate a few real-life e-disaster stories to make the organization's risks come alive. You'll find examples of chilling e-disasters in the pages of this book, through the resources listed in the endnotes and appendices, and in daily newspapers and weekly news magazines.

4. Distribute printed copies of the organization's e-mail rules and e-mail policies. Walk employees through each rule and

policy, point by point. Encourage questions and discussion. Have experts from your legal, IT, and HR departments on hand to answer questions and address concerns.

5. Do not wrap up training until you are certain every employee understands each e-mail rule and policy and is clear on what constitutes appropriate and inappropriate use of the organization's computer assets.

6. Discuss e-mail ownership, privacy expectations, copyright concerns, and confidentiality breaches. If your policies include the monitoring of employee e-mail use, say so.

7. If you allow personal e-mail use, explain to employees exactly what type of personal use is acceptable and unacceptable. Also let your workforce know when personal communication is allowed, for how long, and under what circumstances. If employees are allowed to make personal use of IM, LISTSERVs, and other e-communication technologies, spell out those guidelines, too.

   If you're wondering how other employers handle personal e-mail use, a survey of the American Management Association, *US News & World Report*, and The ePolicy Institute shows that 40 percent of large employers allow full and unrestricted personal use; 21 percent allow full personal use with prior management approval; 7 percent restrict personal use to emergency situations; 4 percent allow personal communication with spouse/family only; and 24 percent outlaw personal use altogether.[2]

   Remember, clear guidelines are always easier to follow. If "some" personal use is allowed, employees and managers will have to interpret where the line is drawn.

8. Review penalties thoroughly. Make it clear that policy violations will result in disciplinary action or termination. If you have assigned specific penalties to certain violations, spell them out for the managers who will have to enforce the policies.

9. Ask each employee to sign and date a copy of the e-mail policy, acknowledging that the employee has read it, understands it, and agrees to comply with it. Employee acknowl-

edgment will help protect the organization from claims by violators who say they had no knowledge of the e-mail rules and policies that led to their termination.

10. Provide each employee with a signed copy of each policy. Put a master set of written e-mail rules and policies in the organization's comprehensive employee handbook. And make electronic copies available via the company's Intranet system as well.

Continuing Education Is Directly Linked to Success

To ensure e-mail policy compliance and success, integrate a program of continuing education. Develop ongoing methods to reinforce training among executives, managers, and employees. Send policy reminders via e-mail. Hold periodic training sessions to update employees on new rules and policy changes. Make annual e-mail policy training mandatory for all executives and staff. Post policy updates on the company's Intranet site.

In short, do whatever it takes to raise employees' e-consciousness, keeping them focused on their role in making the company's e-risk management initiative a success.

Recap and E-Action Plan

E-Mail Rule #37: Employee Compliance Is Key to E-Risk Management Success

1. To be successful, your organization's e-mail rules and policies must be embraced by your employees.

2. Your employees have the right to work in an environment free from harassment, discrimination, and hostility of any kind.

3. Notify employees of the organization's e-mail rules and policies in person.

4. Be sure that every employee understands each e-mail rule and policy and is clear on what constitutes appropriate and inappropriate use of the organization's computer assets.

5. Require each employee to sign and date a copy of every e-mail rule and policy, acknowledging that the employee has read, understands, and will comply with the policy—or accept the consequences, up to and including termination.

6. Make it easy for employees to access e-mail rules and policies. Provide each employee with signed copies of all rules and policies and keep master copies in the comprehensive employee handbook.

7. Create continuing education activities and tools to reinforce training and ensure e-mail rule and policy compliance.

Notes

Chapter 1

1. Richard Power, "2002 CSI/FBI Computer Crime and Security Survey," *Computer Security Issues & Trends,* vol. 8, no. 1 (spring 2002), 4.
2. Alexei Barrionuevo and Jonathan Weil, "Duncan Knew Enron Papers Would Be Lost," *Wall Street Journal* (May 14, 2002), C1.
3. Ann Carrns, "Prying Times: Those Bawdy E-Mails Were Good for a Laugh Until the Ax Fell," *Wall Street Journal* (February 4, 2000), A1, col. 1.
4. Keith Naughton, "CyberSlacking," *Newsweek* (November 29, 1999), 64.
5. "2001 AMA, *US News,* ePolicy Institute Survey: Electronic Policies and Practices," conducted by the American Management Association, *US News & World Report,* and The ePolicy Institute. Survey findings available online at www.epolicyinstitute.com.
6. Power, "2002 CSI/FBI Computer Crime and Security Survey," 4.
7. "2001 AMA, *US News,* ePolicy Institute Survey: Electronic Policies and Practices."
8. Power, "2002 CSI/FBI Computer Crime and Security Survey," 16.
9. Ibid., 4.
10. Elizabeth Weinstein, "Help! I'm Drowning in E-Mail!" *Wall Street Journal* (January 10, 2002), B1.
11. "2001 AMA, *US News,* ePolicy Institute Survey: Electronic Policies and Practices."

Chapter 2

1. "2001 AMA, *US News,* ePolicy Institute Survey: Electronic Policies and Practices."
2. Ibid.

3. See Nancy L. Flynn, *The ePolicy Handbook: Designing and Implementing Effective E-Mail, Internet, and Software Policies* (New York: AMA-COM, 2001).
4. International Association of Administrative Professionals (IAAP) and The ePolicy Institute Online Poll (January 23, 2002).
5. *Faragher v. City of Boca Raton*, 524 U.S. 775 (1998); and *Burlington Industries, Inc. v. Ellerth*, 524 U.S. 742 (1998).

Chapter 3

1. "2001 AMA, *US News*, ePolicy Institute Survey: Electronic Policies and Practices." Survey findings available online at www.epolicyinstitute.com.
2. Richard Power, "2002 CSI/FBI Computer Crime and Security Survey," *Computer Security Issues & Trends*, vol. 8, no. 1 (spring 2002), 6–7.
3. Elron Software, "1999 E-Mail Abuse Study." Findings available online at www.elronsoftware.com.
4. "Man Pleads Guilty to Stealing Trade Secret," press release, U.S. Department of Justice, Eric Melgren, United States Attorney, District of Kansas (June 3, 2002).
5. "Santa Clara Man Sentenced for Theft of Trade Secrets," press release, U.S. Department of Justice, United States Attorney, Northern District of California (December 4, 2001).

Chapter 4

1. Gregory S. Johnson, "A Practitioner's Overview of Digital Discovery," *Gonzaga Law Review* 33, no. 2 (1998), 347.
2. *Monotype Corporation v. International Typeface Corporation*, 43 F. 3d 443 (1994).

Chapter 5

1. "2001 AMA, *US News*, ePolicy Institute Survey: Electronic Policies and Practices." Survey findings available online at www.epolicyinstitute.com.
2. *Smythe v. Pillsbury*, 914 F. Supp. 97 (ED Pa. 1996).

Chapter 6

1. See Nancy L. Flynn, *The ePolicy Handbook: Designing and Implementing Effective E-Mail, Internet, and Software Policies* (New York: AMA-COM, 2001).
2. Ibid.

Chapter 7

1. Ibid.
2. "2001 AMA, *US News*, ePolicy Institute Survey: Electronic Policies and Practices." Survey findings available online at www.epolicyinstitute.com.

Chapter 8

1. Nancy L. Flynn, *The ePolicy Handbook: Designing and Implementing Effective E-Mail, Internet, and Software Policies* (New York: AMACOM, 2001).
2. "2001 AMA, *US News*, ePolicy Institute Survey: Electronic Policies and Practices." Survey findings available online at www.epolicyinstitute.com.
3. Ibid.
4. Edward Wong, "A Stinging Office Memo Boomerangs," *New York Times* (April 5, 2001), C1.

Chapter 9

1. "LISTSERV TODAY," www.lsoft.com. Statistics updated November 14, 2002.

Chapter 10

1. Richard Power, "2002 CSI/FBI Computer Crime and Security Survey," *Computer Security Issues & Trends*, vol. 8, no. 1 (spring 2002), 10.
2. Randolph A. Kahn, "Corralling Electronic Information: Does Your Company Need a Rancher?" *e-doc Magazine* (September/October 2000).
3. International Association of Administrative Professionals (IAAP) and The ePolicy Institute Online Poll (January 23, 2002).

Chapter 11

1. *Faragher v. City of Boca Raton*, 524 U.S. 775(1998); *Burlington Industries, Inc. v. Ellereth*, 524 U.S. 742 (1998).

Chapter 12

1. Elizabeth Weinstein, "Help! I'm Drowning in E-Mail!" *Wall Street Journal* (January 10, 2002), B1.

Chapter 13

1. "2001 AMA, *US News*, ePolicy Institute Survey: Electronic Policies and Practices." Survey findings available online at www.epolicyinstitute.com.

Chapter 15

1. SEC 17 CFR 240.17a-4.
2. Ibid.

Chapter 16

1. *Linnen v. A.H. Robbins Company, Inc. et al.*, WL 462014 (Mass. Super., 1999).
2. *Murphy Oil USA v. Fluor Daniel, Inc.*, WL 246439 (ED La., 2002).
3. *Anti-Monopoly, Inc. v. Hasbro, Inc.*, WL 649934 (S.D.N.Y., 1995).
4. *Public Citizen, et al., v. John Carlin, Archivist of the United States, et al.*, No. 97-5356 (DC CIR., 1999).

Chapter 18

1. Dylan Tweney, "The Defogger: How to Beat the High Cost of Storage," *eCompany Now* (July 2001), 84–85.

Chapter 19

1. *Moore v. General Motors Corp.*, 558 S.W.2d 720, 736 (Mo. Ct. App. 1977).

Chapter 20

1. *Bills v. Kennecott Corp.*, 108 F.R.D. 459, 462 (D. Utah 1985).
2. Electronic Signatures in Global and National Commerce Act, Pub. L. No. 106-229.
3. ESIGN § 101(d).
4. UETA § Section 12.
5. IRS Procedure 97-22.

Chapter 21

1. Randolph A. Kahn and Diane Silverberg, "From Mount Sinai to Cyberspace: Making Good E-Business Records," *The Business Lawyer* 57 (No-

vember 2001), 431–45; Randolph A. Kahn, "Making Your Technologist an Electronic Record Builder," *e-Doc Magazine* 15 (November/December 2001), 30.
2. *Illinois v. Bovio*, 453 NE 2d 829, 1983.
3. *Monotype Corporation v. International Typeface Corporation*, 43 F. 3d 443 (1994).
4. *Knox v. State of Indiana*, 93 F. 3d (7th Cir., 1996).

Chapter 22

1. *Bills v. Kennecott Corp.*, 108 F.R.D. 459, 462 (D. Utah, 1985).
2. FED. RUL. CIV. PROC. 34(a).
3. FED. RUL. CIV. PROC. 26 (a)(1)(B).
4. *Toledo Fair Hous. Ctr. v. Nationwide Mut. Ins. Co.*, 703 N.E.2d 340 (Ohio C.P., 1996).
5. *Anti-Monopoly, Inc. v. Hasbro, Inc.*, 1995 WL 649934 (S.D.N.Y., 1995).
6. Ibid.; and *American Brass, et al., v. United States, et al.*, 12 C.I.T. 1068, 699 F. Supp. 934 (1988).
7. *United States of America v. Samuel Waksal* (02 Cr. Indictment).
8. *Danis v. USN Communications, Inc.*, 2000 WL 1694325 (N.D.Ill., 2000).
9. *In re Brand Name Prescription Drugs Antitrust Litigation*, 1995 WL 360526 (N.D.Ill., 1995).
10. *Anti-Monopoly, Inc. v. Hasbro, Inc.*, 1995 WL 649934 (S.D.N.Y., 1995).
11. *Sattar v. Motorola*, 138 F.3d 1164 (7th Cir., 1997).
12. James M. Rosenbaum, "In Defense of the Delete Key," *The Green Bag*, vol. 3, no. 4, 2nd series (summer 2000), 5.

Chapter 23

1. Randolph A. Kahn and Kristi L. Vaiden, "If the Slate Is Wiped Clean. Spoliation: What It Can Mean for Your Case," *Business Law Today*, vol. 8, no. 5 (May/June 1999).
2. *Mathias v. Jacobs*, 197 F.R.D. 29 (S.D.N.Y., 2000).
3. Alexei Barrionuevo and Jonathan Weil, "Duncan Knew Enron Papers Would Be Lost," *Wall Street Journal* (May 14, 2002), C1.

Chapter 25

1. *Danis v. USN Communications, Inc.*, 2000 WL 1694325 (N.D.Ill., 2000) provides an excellent overview of an organization's responsibilities in the face of audits, investigations, and litigation.

The court enumerated the CEO's failures as follows:

1. The CEO "personally took no affirmative steps to ensure that the [document retention] directive was followed."
2. He did not direct that the company "implement a written, comprehensive document preservation policy, either in general or with specific reference to the lawsuit";
3. "he did not instruct that any e-mail or other written communication be sent to staff to ensure that they were aware of the lawsuit and the need to preserve documents";
4. "and he did not meet with the department heads after this staff meeting to follow up to see what they had done to implement the document preservation directive . . ."
5. He "exhibited extraordinarily poor judgment" by delegating these responsibilities to an in-house attorney with no litigation experience nor experience in developing a retention program, when he had the option of using the outside law firm, with a deep experience in the area.
    a. The in-house attorney erred by doing "nothing to ensure that all . . . employees who handled documents that might be discoverable were aware of the lawsuit and the need to preserve documents:
    b. "he held no meetings with employees below the managerial level,"
    c. "and he did not issue any written communications to anyone on the subject . . ."
    d. "[He] did nothing to determine whether the managers who attended the staff meeting followed his direction of communicating to their respective departments the need to preserve documents . . ."
    e. "[He] did not review the pre-existing practices . . . relating to document preservation for terminated employees and closed offices, to determine whether these practices were still suitable in light of the need to preserve documents as a result of litigation."
2. *In re Dow Corning Corp.*, 250 B.R. 298 (Bkrtcy.E.D. Mich., 2000).

Chapter 26

1. John Schwartz, "Year After 9/11, Cyberspace Door Is Still Ajar," *New York Times* (September 9, 2002), technology sec., 1
2. 21 CFR Part 11 § 11.10 (e) (1997).
3. 21 CFR Part 11 § 11.10 (g).

Chapter 27

1. Richard Power, "2002 CSI/FBI Computer Crime and Security Survey," *Computer Security Issues & Trends,* vol. 8, no. 1 (spring 2002), 10.

Chapter 28

1. Thomas Raschke, "Policy-Based Content Security," IDC white paper sponsored by Clearswift (2001), www.clearswift.com.

Chapter 31

1. Nancy Flynn, "Managing E-Mail Overload: Expert Tips to Help You Get a Grip on Spam," white paper sponsored by Elron Software, www.elron-software.com (November 2002).
2. Robert W. Ahrens, "Spam Alert," *USA Today Snapshots*® (September 6, 2002), A1. Source: Brightmail survey.
3. Flynn, "Managing E-Mail Overload."
4. "Reduce the Effects of Unwanted E-Mail," *eBusiness Advisor* (June 1, 2002).
5. Thomas Raschke, "Policy-Based Content Security," IDC white paper sponsored by Clearswift (2001), www.clearswift.com.
6. Flynn, "Managing E-Mail Overload."
7. Keith Naughton, "CyberSlacking," *Newsweek* (November 29, 1999), 65.
8. "2001 Corporate Web and Email Usage Study," Elron Software.
9. Meta Group research cited in "Effective Spam Management," Clearswift white paper (September 2002).
10. Raschke, "Policy-Based Content Security."
11. "Effective Spam Management," Clearswift white paper (September 2002), www.clearswift.com.
12. International Association of Administrative Professionals (IAAP) and The ePolicy Institute Online Poll (January 23, 2002).

Chapter 32

1. Tim McDonald, "Instant Messaging Enterprise Security Ramps Up," *NewsFactor Network* (May 31, 2002).
2. Ibid.
3. Ibid.
4. Frank Thorsberg, "Is IM a Sieve for Corporate Secrets?" *PCWorld.com* (July 19, 2002).
5. Ibid.
6. Brian Sullivan, "Intruders Target Instant Messaging: CERT Security Service Cites Bogus Warnings That Actually Sabotage Messaging," *Computerworld* (March 20, 2002).

Chapter 33

1. Simon Buckingham, "SMS in North America Crosses 1 Billion Messages a Month Mark," *Mobile Streams* report (July 9, 2002).

2. Richard Shim, "BlackBerry Maker Struggling to Blossom," C|NET News-.com (May 9, 2002).
3. Mark S. Thompson, "The Future of SMS," The PELORUS Group report (May 2002).
4. Buckingham, "SMS in North America."
5. Adam Stone, "SMS Is Back Big-Time for Corporations and Consumers," *Instant Messaging Planet* (May 3, 2002).

Chapter 34

1. Joe Wilcox, "Microsoft Says No to Music Swapping," C|NET News.com (July 26, 2002).

Chapter 36

1. Nancy L. Flynn, *The ePolicy Handbook: Designing and Implementing Effective E-Mail, Internet, and Software Policies* (New York: AMACOM, 2001).

Chapter 37

1. Ibid.
2. "2001 AMA, *US News*, ePolicy Institute Survey: Electronic Policies and Practices." Survey findings available online at www.epolicyinstitute.com.

Appendix A: Sample Rules

Rule: Retention of E-Mail Records for Paper-Based Retention

All e-mail messages (whether in electronic form or printed on paper) that have an ongoing legal, compliance, business, or operational value (considered a "record") or relate to an audit, investigation, or litigation must be retained in accordance with the company's records management policies and applicable retention schedules. It is the responsibility of every e-mail user to help maintain e-mail records.

It is the responsibility of each user to retain e-mail records (defined as any e-mail having an ongoing legal, compliance, business, operational, or historical value) like all other records in accordance with the company's retention policies. You are to manage and retain e-mail records by printing a copy of the e-mail with all transmission information (sender, recipient[s], date, routing data, etc.) and securely storing a copy in paper form as the official copy in a paper folder with all other records on the same or similar topic.

The company's active e-mail system, e-mail servers, archives, electronic folders, and/or in-boxes will no longer serve as locations for storage and retrieval of e-mail. The primary location for retention of e-mail records will be in paper folders within the area surrounding your workspace.

To maximize the operating efficiency of the company's e-mail system and to minimize the storage costs associated with retaining large volumes of unnecessary e-mail, any e-mail stored in an e-mail account in-box or any related electronic folder will automatically be purged after ___ days. E-mail will be backed up for disaster recovery purposes on a weekly basis and will thereafter be retained for ___ months. If you will not be able to access your e-mail account for more than ___ days, please contact _____ to make arrangements for your e-mail account during your absence.

If you have any questions about the above policies, address them to _____ before signing the following agreement.

I have read _____'s Retention of E-Mail Records Rule and agree to abide by it. I understand that violation of any of the above policies and procedures may result in disciplinary action, up to and including my termination.

_____

User Name

_____

User Signature

_____

Date

©2003, Nancy Flynn and Randolph Kahn, Esq. For informational purposes only. Get the advice of counsel before taking any action regarding records retention.

Rule: Dispose of Nonrecord E-Mail Messages

All copies of nonrecord e-mail (those with no ongoing legal, compliance, business, operational, or historical value) should be deleted and paper printouts of such messages disposed of when no longer needed. Nonrecord e-mail messages include, but are not limited to, administrative e-mail (such as an invitation to the company holiday party or a meeting notice); they may not need to be retained as a company record, according to the records retention schedule. Such messages only need to be kept as long as they're needed to conduct business. Failure to dispose of such messages wastes valuable company computer resources and employee time. However, if you would retain the message if it had been sent in paper form, then you should retain the e-mail transmission.

I have read _____'s Dispose of Nonrecord E-Mail Messages Rule and agree to abide by it. I understand that violation of any of the above policies and procedures may result in disciplinary action, up to and including my termination.

_____

User Name

_____

User Signature

_____

Date

©2003, Nancy Flynn and Randolph Kahn, Esq. For informational purposes only. Get the advice of counsel before taking any action regarding nonrecords disposal.

Employee Retention Rules

You are responsible for properly retaining e-mail that qualifies as a business record and disposing of all other e-mail messages. You should, unless otherwise directed:

1. Purge drafts and nonrecord e-mail messages immediately when they are no longer needed.

2. Purge convenience or reference e-mail copies immediately when they are no longer needed.

3. Purge duplicates immediately when they are no longer needed.

I have read _____'s Employee Retention Rules and agree to abide by them. I understand any violation of any of the above policies and procedures may result in disciplinary action, up to and including my termination.

_____

User Name

_____

User Signature

_____

Date

Appendix B: Sample E-Mail Policies

E-Mail Policy 1

(Organization) is pleased to make e-mail access available to authorized employees. Created as a business tool to help (Organization) employees serve customers, communicate with suppliers, streamline internal communications, and reduce unnecessary paperwork, the e-mail system is intended primarily for business purposes. Personal use of (Organization's) e-mail system is restricted to the terms outlined below. The e-mail system is the property of (Organization). Employees accessing (Organization's) e-mail system are required to adhere to the following policy and procedures. Violation of (Organization's) e-mail policy may result in disciplinary action, up to and including termination.

1. All communications and information transmitted, received, or archived in (Organization's) computer system belong to the company. The law gives management the right to access and disclose all employee e-mail messages transmitted or received via the organization's computer system. (Organization) may exercise its legal right to monitor employees' e-mail activity. When it comes to e-mail, employees should have no expectation of privacy. Be aware that management

may access and monitor e-mail at any time for any reason without notice.

2. The e-mail system is reserved primarily for business use. Only under the following circumstances may employees use (Organization's) e-mail system for personal reasons:

   a. Communication with children, spouses, domestic partners, and immediate family is permitted but must be limited to no more than 15 minutes a day during business hours. Employees also are free to e-mail children, spouses, domestic partners, and immediate family during the lunch hour and other authorized break times. [*Some companies may want to restrict even this limited amount of personal use within their e-mail policy.*]

   b. Personal e-mail communication that exceeds the time limits outlined in point 2a and/or that is conducted between the employee and an individual other than a child, spouse, domestic partner, or immediate family member is prohibited unless authorized by (Organization's) human resources manager.

   c. The use of (Organization's) e-mail system to solicit for any purpose, campaign for a political candidate, espouse political views, promote a religious cause, and/or advertise the sale of merchandise is strictly prohibited without the prior approval of the Chief Information Officer.

3. E-mail passwords are the property of (Organization). Employees are required to provide the Chief Information Officer with current passwords. Only authorized personnel are permitted to use passwords to access another employee's e-mail without consent. Misuse of passwords, the sharing of passwords with nonemployees, and/or the unauthorized use of another employee's password will result in disciplinary action, up to and including termination.

4. Privacy is difficult if not impossible to achieve in the electronic age. Confidential or personal information never should be sent via e-mail without the understanding that it can be intercepted. This includes the transmission of customer financial information, Social Security numbers, em-

ployee health records, proprietary data and trade secrets, and/or other confidential material. When sending confidential material (or any messages, for that matter), employees should use extreme caution to ensure that the intended recipient's e-mail address is correct.

5. Exercise sound judgment and common sense when distributing e-mail messages. Client-related messages should be carefully guarded and protected, like any other written materials. You must also abide by copyright laws, ethics rules, and other applicable laws. Exercise caution when sending blind carbon copies to ensure that you don't violate addressees' privacy by inadvertently sending carbon copies.

6. E-mail usage must conform with (Organization's) harassment and discrimination policies. Messages containing defamatory, obscene, menacing, threatening, offensive, harassing, or otherwise objectionable and/or inappropriate statements—and/or messages that disclose personal information without authorization—are prohibited. If you receive this type of prohibited, unsolicited message, do not forward it. Notify your supervisor, the law department, and/or the Chief Information Officer about the message. Handle the message as instructed by management.

7. E-mail messages should be treated as formal business documents, written in accordance with (Organization's) guidelines. Style, spelling, grammar, and punctuation should be appropriate and accurate, and the rules of netiquette must be adhered to.

8. Employees are prohibited from sending jokes, rumors, gossip, or unsubstantiated opinions via e-mail. These communications, which often contain objectionable material, are easily misconstrued when communicated electronically.

9. Employees are prohibited from sending organization-wide e-mail messages to all employees without approval from the law department or Chief Information Officer. In addition, employees are prohibited from requesting e-mail replies to organization-wide e-mail without the permission of the Chief Information Officer.

10. Employees may not waste (Organization's) computer resources or colleagues' time. Send e-mail messages and copies only to those with a legitimate need to read your message. Chain messages and executable graphics should be deleted, not forwarded, as they can overload the system.

11. Only the Chief Information Officer and/or systems administrator may generate public mail distribution lists.

12. Employees are responsible for knowing and adhering to (Organization's) e-mail retention and deletion policies.

13. Misuse and/or abuse of (Organization's) electronic assets (wasting productive time online, copying or downloading copyrighted materials, visiting inappropriate sites, sending inappropriate/abusive e-mail messages, etc.) will result in disciplinary action, up to and including termination.

If you have any questions about the above policies, address them to _____ before signing the following agreement.

I have read _____'s E-Mail Policy and agree to abide by it. I understand that violation of any of the above policies and procedures may result in disciplinary action, up to and including my termination.

_____

User Name

_____

User Signature

_____

Date
©2003, Nancy Flynn and Randolph Kahn, Esq. For informational purposes only. Get the advice of counsel before taking any action regarding e-mail policy.

E-Mail Policy 2

Because e-mail is an efficient way to send urgent messages and/ or messages to multiple readers, _____ is pleased to make e-mail access available to employees. Employees using the organization's e-mail system must adhere to the following e-mail policy and procedures:

1. The e-mail system is reserved for business use only.

2. Use extreme caution to ensure that the correct e-mail address is used for the intended recipient(s).

3. Be aware that management may access and monitor e-mail at any time for any reason without notice.

4. Do not treat e-mail as confidential or private.

5. Employees must provide the Chief Information Officer with passwords.

6. Only authorized personnel are permitted to access another person's e-mail without consent.

7. Employees should exercise sound judgment and common sense when distributing messages. Client-related messages should be carefully guarded and protected, like any other written materials. You also must abide by copyright laws, ethics rules, and other applicable laws.

8. Sending harassing, abusive, intimidating, discriminatory, or other offensive e-mails is strictly prohibited.

9. Use of _____'s e-mail system to solicit for any purpose without the consent of the Chief Information Officer is strictly prohibited.

10. Violation of this e-mail policy will subject the employee to disciplinary action, up to and including termination.

If you have any questions about the above policies, address them to _____ before signing the following agreement.

I have read _____'s E-Mail Policy and agree to abide by it. I understand that violation of any of the above policies and procedures may result in disciplinary action, up to and including my termination.

_____

User Name

_____

User Signature

_____

Date

E-Mail Policy 3

This policy provides employees with effective, consistent e-mail usage standards. This policy applies to all employees of the company at all locations.

▪ All communications and information transmitted, received, or archived in the company's computer system belong to the company. The company reserves the right to access and disclose all employee e-mail messages.

▪ E-mail messages should be treated as formal documents. Style, spelling, grammar, and punctuation should be appropriate and accurate.

▪ Use professional, appropriate language in e-mail messages. Employees are prohibited from sending abusive, harassing, threatening, or otherwise offensive messages.

▪ Employees are prohibited from sending jokes, rumors, gossip, or unsubstantiated opinions via e-mail. These communications, which often contain objectionable material, are easily misconstrued when communicated electronically.

▪ Be aware that privacy does not exist in cyberspace. Never transmit confidential or personal information via e-mail.

▪ Employees are prohibited from sending organization-wide e-mail messages to all employees without approval from the Chief Information Officer.

▪ Employees may not waste computer resources or colleagues' time. Send e-mail messages and copies only to those with a legitimate need to read your message.

■ Adhere to netiquette guidelines as detailed in the organization's electronic writing style manual.

If you have any questions about the above policies, address them to _____ before signing the following agreement.

I have read _____'s e-mail policy and agree to abide by it. I understand that violation of any of the above policies and procedures may result in disciplinary action, up to and including my termination.

_____

User Name

_____

User Signature

_____

Date

©2003, Nancy Flynn and Randolph Kahn, Esq. For informational purposes only. Get the advice of counsel before taking any action regarding e-mail policy.

Appendix C: Resources and Expert Sources

E-Mail, Electronic Records, and Retention Policy Development and Training

Kahn Consulting, Inc.
Randolph A. Kahn, Esq.
157 Leonard Wood North
Highland Park, IL 60035
847-266-0722
www.KahnConsultingInc.com

Kahn Consulting, Inc., is a consulting firm specializing in the legal, risk management, and policy issues of information management and electronic records. Through a range of services, including information management and e-records policy development, risk management audits, policy and practice audit and evaluation, product assessments, legal and compliance research, and education and training, KCI helps its clients address today's critical issues in an ever-changing regulatory and technological environment. To book a consultation, speaker, or media interview, contact RKahn@KahnConsultingInc.com or visit: www.KahnConsultingInc.com.

E-Policy Development, Implementation, and Training

The ePolicy Institute™
Nancy Flynn, Executive Director
2300 Walhaven Ct., Suite 200A
Columbus, OH 43220
614/451-3200
www.epolicyinstitute.com

The ePolicy Institute helps employers reduce e-risks, while helping employees enhance e-communications. A leading source of e-policy, e-mail management, and e-mail writing training tools and services, The ePolicy Institute operates an international Speakers' Bureau and conducts on-site and online training. Executive Director and author Nancy Flynn, a noted authority on e-policy and e-mail, has been featured in the *Wall Street Journal, US News & World Report*, National Public Radio, and thousands of media outlets worldwide. To book a consultation, speaker, or media interview, contact nancy@epolicyinstitute .com or visit www.epolicyinstitute.com.

E-Mail Writing, E-Mail Management, and Netiquette Training

The ePolicy Institute™
Nancy Flynn, Executive Director
2300 Walhaven Ct., Suite 200A
Columbus, OH 43220
614/451-3200
www.epolicyinstitute.com

The ePolicy Institute helps employers reduce e-risks, while helping employees enhance e-communications. A leading source of e-policy, e-mail management, and e-mail writing training tools and services, The ePolicy Institute operates an international Speakers' Bureau and conducts on-site and online training. Executive Director and author Nancy Flynn, a noted authority on e-policy and e-mail, has been featured in the *Wall Street Journal, US News & World Report*, National Public Radio, and thousands of media outlets worldwide. To book a consultation, speaker, or media interview, contact nancy@epolicyinstitute .com or visit www.epolicyinstitute.com.

Legal, Risk Management, and Policy Issues of Information Technology

Kahn Consulting, Inc.
Randolph A. Kahn, Esq.
157 Leonard Wood North
Highland Park, IL 60035
847-266-0722
www.KahnConsultingInc.com

Kahn Consulting, Inc., is a consulting firm specializing in the legal and policy issues of information management and electronic records. Through a range of services, including information management and e-records policy development, risk management audits, policy and practice audit and evaluation, product assessments, legal and compliance research, and education and training, KCI helps its clients address today's critical issues in an ever-changing regulatory and technological environment. To book a consultation, speaker, or media interview, contact RKahn@KahnConsultingInc.com or visit www.KahnCon sultingInc.com.

Policy-Based Content Security

Clearswift Corporation
15500 SE 30th Place
Suite 200
Bellevue, WA 98007
426-460-6000
www.clearswift.com

Clearswift is the world's leading provider of software for managing and securing electronic communications, with a 23 percent share of the global content filtering market. Clearswift delivers the capabilities for organizations to protect themselves against e-mail and Web-based threats, meet legal and regulatory requirements, implement productivity-saving policies, and manage intellectual property passing through their network.

The company's expertise lies in establishing and enforcing e-policies. Content security threats include the circulation of inappropriate images and text, spam, oversize files, loss and corruption of data, and breaches of confidentiality, as well as viruses and malicious code. Clearswift's software portfolio includes Clearswift MIMEsweeper, a product family for e-mail and Web e-policies, and Clearswift ENTERPRISEsuite, a software infrastructure for managing e-policies in complex environments. More information about Clearswift, its products, and services is available at www.clearswift.com.

ClearBase, ClearEdge, ClearPoint, Clearswift ENTER-PRISEsuite, Clearswift ES, ES Bastion, ES Director Options, ES for Service Providers, ES X.400 Filter, e-Sweeper, MAILsweeper, MIMEsweeper, PORNsweeper, SECRETsweeper, and WEBsweeper are all registered trademarks of Clearswift.

E-Mail Archiving and Records Management

Iron Mountain Digital Archives
800-899-IRON
www.ironmountain.com

Iron Mountain is the world's leading provider of records management and information protection services, operating in eighty U.S. markets and serving more than 150,000 customer accounts. Iron Mountain has also achieved significant international growth and currently serves customers in forty-four markets in Europe, Canada, and Latin America. Whether you need long-term archiving and access to electronic records or you need to ensure that your backup data is always current and available for recovery, Iron Mountain Digital Services has the solution. Iron Mountain offers both short-term vaulting of backup data for fast-changing transactional data and long-term archiving of valuable digital assets, including e-mail, scanned images, and electronic statements and reports. To learn more, visit: www.ironmountain.com.

E-Mail Management and Archiving

Legato Systems, Inc.
2350 West El Camino Real
Mountain View, CA 94040
650-210-7000
www.legato.com

LEGATO delivers enterprise-class software and services that protect and manage information, assure the availability of applications, and provide immediate access to business-critical information. Supporting Microsoft Exchange, Lotus Notes, Unix Sendmail, and Bloomberg Mail, LEGATO's EmailXtender® family of e-mail management and archiving solutions is a comprehensive, policy-based system that automatically collects, organizes, retains, and retrieves messages/attachments. By creating and managing a central repository of e-mail and other messages, EmailXtender helps reduce the cost of e-mail storage, boost end-user and administrator productivity, and control risk by supporting compliance with government regulations. The EmailXtender family works in conjunction with LEGATO's Availability and Information Protection solutions to help boost operational efficiency and ensure business continuity by automating e-mail management, protecting the messaging system, and keeping it available.

Appendix D: Glossary of E-Mail, Legal, and Technical Terms

■ **ASP (Application Service Provider).** A third-party "outsourced" business that provides software applications as a service over a network for a recurring fee, as opposed to the traditional software licensing model that entails a one-time license purchase and local installation and operation. Various types of software and services can be "rented" in this way. Some companies are attracted to the ASP model because it does not require a major capital investment upfront, and ongoing application service and maintenance are handled by the ASP. For example, ASPs now exist to store and archive enterprise e-mail.

Note: ASP is also used as an acronym for Active Server Pages, an unrelated Web technology.

■ **Asymmetric encryption.** A type of encryption employed by Public Key Infrastructure that uses different keys for encryption and decryption. Unlike symmetric encryption, which uses the same key for both purposes, in asymmetric encryption there is no need to keep the encryption key secret. This eliminates the problem of securely distributing the encryption/decryption key to each message sender and recipient, which makes it ideally suited to Internet applications.

■ **Audit trail.** Information about a document's possession, control, access, alteration, authorship, disposition, etc. This trail of information is useful for a variety of business and legal purposes (in cases of fraud, for example) because it can be used to show who had control of a document at a certain time. Audit trail information can come from a variety of sources, including server log files, handwritten notes, policies and practices, direct testimony, and information on the document itself about authorship and ownership.

■ **Authenticity.** Records, evidence, and other information are said to be authentic if their authors and content can be conclusively verified and demonstrated to be original. In other words, an authentic document is in fact what it purports to be.

■ **Business record.** Evidence of business activities, events, and transactions that organizations retain because the information has ongoing business, legal, compliance, operational, or historical value.

■ **Classification.** The act of sorting business records into categories determined by the record's content. Also referred to as "coding" or "categorization." Classification is important for ensuring that records are retained for the period of time required by business practice or law.

■ **Digital signature.** A specific type of electronic signature that uses special software to create a unique digital fingerprint of a document (called a "hash") that can subsequently be used to verify that the contents of the document have not been changed and demonstrate who the original signer was. Digital signatures are typically used within the context of Public Key Infrastructure (PKI).

■ **Discovery.** The process by which information is learned from your adversary and evidence is collected and produced for litigation. Discovery is the part of the legal process that involves parties on each side exchanging documents, taking depositions, answering questions, taking testimony, and exchanging information that helps them build their case and prepare for the proceeding. Discovery prevents parties from being "ambushed" with unexpected information and helps each side understand the material facts and evidence in advance of the proceeding.

■ **Embedded information.** In the information management context, "data within data" that may not be obvious or easy to access and retain and thus provides one of the many unique challenges of managing digital information. Word processing documents can typically include a variety of nontextual information such as spreadsheet tables and images that may rely on additional programs or information for access.

■ **Encryption.** A mathematical process performed by special software for scrambling plain text and other digital information in such a way that it can only be unscrambled and read by a person with the ability to decrypt. The scrambling process is called "encrypting," and the unscrambling process "decrypting." There are many ways to encrypt information, including asymmetric encryption.

■ **Filtering.** In the information security context, the act of scanning the entry or exit of digital information and stopping content that may be harmful, violate a predetermined rule, or is otherwise undesirable. For example, antivirus software uses a form of filtering to scan incoming e-mail for attachments and other data that may contain malicious codes, such as viruses and worms. In the information management context, filtering can also be used as a form of classification.

■ **Firewall.** A piece of hardware or a software program that automatically examines network traffic and either blocks it or allows it to pass based upon predefined rules and security policies. Firewalls typically sit between a private internal network and the Internet and are one of the most common tools for protecting internal networks and users from harmful content and intrusion.

■ **Hearsay.** Normally, when hearing evidence in a case, the courts consider direct testimony from an individual who was a witness to, or has firsthand knowledge of, an event, as their testimony is considered likely to be the most accurate and trustworthy. The court will normally not admit "hearsay" evidence, such as testimony from one person that simply recounts what another person said. On their own, business records are a form of hearsay. Unless those who "touched" a business record during its lifecycle are called to testify, there is no firsthand testimony about the record.

However, the courts long ago realized that business records

are an important source of evidence and have therefore created an exception to the prohibition on hearsay, which is commonly referred to as the "Business Records Exception to the Hearsay Rule." This exception (and there are many others) allows business records that are created and kept in the "ordinary course of business," to be admitted into court.

▓ **IP (Internet Protocol).** The communication method or protocol used to send data from one computer to another over the Internet. Each computer on the Internet has an IP address (analogous to a phone number) that allows routers to find and forward data to the appropriate computers on the Internet.

▓ **IRC (Internet Relay Chat).** One of the methods for real-time, point-to-point messaging (Instant Messaging).

▓ **Legacy system.** Any information system, including software and hardware, that may no longer be fully supported by its manufacturer or the user or has been in use for a long time.

▓ **LISTSERV®.** E-mail list management software provided by L-Soft International, Inc., that is so widely used that the term "LISTSERV" is often used generically to refer to any e-mail-based discussion group. In a typical LISTSERV discussion group, all e-mail sent to a designated e-mail address is forwarded to all subscribers to the discussion group, thereby providing a convenient method for groups of people to communicate.

▓ **Metadata.** Data that describes other data. For example, the index or table of contents in a book could be considered a form of metadata. From a records management or legal perspective, metadata is an integral component of an electronic record.

▓ **Newsgroup.** A newsgroup provides a forum for online discussion through the posting and viewing of text-based messages to topic-based "news groups." Using newsgroups is similar to using e-mail, with the primary difference being that a "sent" message is posted to the newsgroup, where any newsgroup subscriber can read it, instead of directly to an individual recipient. There are thousands of public newsgroups on just about every imaginable topic.

■ **Packet.** Information sent over the Internet is sent in packets, including e-mail messages, that use the TCP/IP protocol (Transmission Control Protocol/Internet Protocol). Software employing this protocol breaks all data down into small packets, sends them across the Internet through various routers, then reassembles the packets at the other end. One packet does not necessarily take the same path as another. In addition, the software can determine if any packets are lost and send them again automatically. The advantage to this system is that a continuous connection between the sending and receiving computers is not required during transmission, which means that several transmissions can occur at the same time, such as in the case of a Web server.

■ **Packet sniffer.** See Sniffer.

■ **PDA (Personal Digital Assistant).** A broad category of handheld hardware devices commonly used in place of an appointment and address book. As PDAs increase in power and speed, their functionality is also growing to include audio/video and wireless e-mail capabilities.

■ **P2P (Peer-to-Peer).** A method for one computer to locate another computer on a network and then communicate directly with it once the connection has been made.

■ **PKI (Public Key Infrastructure).** A system of people, processes, and technology for issuing and managing digital certificates that can be used for online identification, digital signing, encryption, and other information security-related functions.

■ **Records "hold" or litigation hold.** The process of identifying and preserving business records and other information that may be relevant to current or pending litigation, audits, investigations, and other formal proceedings. A failure to adequately preserve such records by notifying employees of their obligations can lead to charges of spoliation or destruction of evidence. Also referred to as a "records hold process."

■ **Router.** A hardware device and/or software application that routes packets of information traveling over the Internet and diverts them to the appropriate location on the Internet, as determined by their destination IP address. A typical e-mail message or other piece of Internet data passes through several routers on its way from sender to recipient.

▪ **SMS (Short Message Service).** A type of text message sent and received from a mobile digital phone.

▪ **Sniffer.** A software application that monitors Internet network traffic by reviewing packets of information as they pass through the network. Sniffers are used by network managers for legitimate purposes such as monitoring networking efficiency and bandwidth use, and also by hackers for illegitimate purposes.

▪ **Spoliation.** The legal term referring to destruction of evidence, intentional or otherwise.

▪ **SSP (Storage Service Provider).** An outsourcing organization similar to an ASP, except that the services provided relate to the storage, archiving, and management of data or information.

▪ **Trojan horse.** A term originating from Greek mythology that in the computer context refers to an apparently harmless software code that actually contains a malicious code. Once installed, the malicious code within the Trojan horse can perform various damaging operations.

▪ **VPN (Virtual Private Network).** A technique for creating a "virtual" private network between two computers by encrypting all information passing back and forth between them. The private network is virtual, because unlike actual private networks, there is no dedicated piece of wire running between the two computers. VPNs are commonly used by organizations to securely give remote employees access to internal networks.

▪ **VoIP (Voice Over IP).** A technique for sending voice data over the Internet using Internet Protocol. In other words, using a computer, microphone, speaker, and Internet connection instead of a telephone. Although the Internet was not designed for this type of communication, several companies provide software and services for VoIP that enable nearly free long distance voice communication.

▪ **Worm.** A type of "person-created" malicious code or computer virus that replicates itself on a computer, using up more and more of the computer's memory and system resources until the computer becomes sluggish or even inoperable.

Appendix E

Recommended Reading

Flynn, Nancy. *The ePolicy Handbook: Designing and Implementing Effective E-Mail, Internet, and Software Policies.* New York: AMACOM, 2001.

Flynn, Nancy, and Tom Flynn. *Writing Effective E-Mail: Improving Your Electronic Communication.* Menlo Park, Calif.: Crisp Publications, Inc., 2003, 1998.

Kahn, Randolph, "Authentic Electronic Evidence: The Need for Trustworthy E-Mail, a Survey of Selected Case Law." Symmetricom White Paper, 2002.

Kahn, Randolph, "A Lawyer's Guide to Digital Information Lifecycle Management," a chapter of *Electronic Information, Its Life Cycle: A Legal Perspective.* Washington, DC: Federal Bar Association, 2002.

Kahn, Randolph, and Barclay T. Blair, "Electronic Discovery: From Novelty to Target." Legato Systems, Inc., Special Report, 2002.

Kahn, Randolph, "Electronic Records: Addressing Legal Admissibility & Recordkeeping Requirements." Iron Mountain, Inc., Guide, 2002.

Kahn, Randolph, and Barclay T. Blair, "Records Management Redefined: From the Backroom to the Boardroom." Legato Systems, Inc., Special Report, 2002.

Kahn, Randolph, "Electronic Records Retention: Managing Messaging Technology Is IT's Problem." *Wall Street & Technology,* October 2002.

Barrett, Michael, and Randolph Kahn, "The Governance of Records Management." *Directors & Boards,* spring 2002.

Kahn, Randolph, and Diane J. Silverberg, "From Mt. Sinai to Cyberspace: Making Good E-Business Records." American Bar Association, *The Business Lawyer,* November 2001.

Kahn, Randolph, "Managing E-Mail Is Essential in Today's Business Environ-

247

ment: Carrots and Sticks Abound to Ensure Companies Manage E-Mail."
Hewlett-Packard White Paper, 2001.

Kahn, Randolph, "E-Discovery Invites Inadvertent Waiver of the Attorney-
Client Privilege." Pike and Fischer, *Digital Discovery & E-Evidence*,
March 2001.

Kahn, Randolph, "Corralling Electronic Information: Does Your Company
Need a Rancher?" *e-doc Magazine*, October 2000.

Note: Readers may access many of the articles and reports referenced here
online at http://www.KahnConsultingInc.com.

Index

administrative assistants, potential
   e-mail misuse by, 17
age discrimination, example of, 57
alternative technologies, 195–197
antispam legislation, 184
antispam software, 183
Application Service Providers (ASPs)
   considerations before using, 97
   definition of, 93
   legal concerns of, 94
   pros and cons of, 94
Arthur Andersen,
   avoidable actions of, 139
   destruction of evidence by, 136
ASPs, *see* Application Service Providers
attachments, use of, 41
attachment warehouse, 103–104
autoclassification
   of e-mail text, 89
   retention issues of, 91
   value of, 90
automation
   e-mail rules for, 92
   and search tools, 170

backup systems, purpose of, 81
backup tapes

disposal of, 82
uses of, 82
BlackBerry, 19
blind carbon copy (bcc), 41, *see also*
   carbon copy
breech, of security, 155
brokerage firms, control over outbound
   e-mail, 169
business records
   assessment for handling, 73–74
   authenticity of, 118
   benefits of transferring, 82–83
   courtroom use of, 119
   definition of, 63, 66
   e-mail as, 28
   example of, 65–66
   identifying e-mail as, 65, 68
   importance of retaining, 63
   important points for, 69
   integrity of, 117
   legal management of, 68–69
   management handling of, 65, 73
   operational values of, 67
   rules for retention of, 75
   training employees to identify,
      101–102
   trustworthiness of, 73

business records (*continued*)
  types of, 64
  qualities of good, 110–111
Business Records Exception to the
    Hearsay Rule, 28, 108, 118–119
business risk factors, 153

capitalization, 42
carbon copy (cc), use of, 41
Carlin, John, 87
cc, *see* carbon copy
centralized forums
  description of, 194
  types of, 194–195
central management, of e-mail, 7
Cerner Corporation, poor use of e-mail
    at, 46–47
Chang, Mikahel K., 21–22
cipher, 176
classification, of e-mail, 7
Clearswift Corp., 238–239
  content security software of, 171
coding, e-mail messages, 99
confidential information, 47
content filtering, 169
  handling unwanted results of, 170
content rules, 27, 29, 168–169
content security, 162–163
  establishing rules for, 168–169
continuing education, 215
corporate espionage, rise of, 21
CRM, *see* Customer Relationship
    Management
Customer Relationship Management
    (CRM), 67

data protection, 7
data theft
  example of, 21
  handling, 23–24
decryption, 176
deletion, of e-mail, 70
denial of service, 165
digital retention, 83–85
digital signature technology, 175
direct e-mail, 202
direct marketing, use of spam in, 180
discovery
  challenges of e-mail in, 126

costs of, 130–131
definition of legal term, 125
employers and, 127–128
lost productivity because of,
    131–132
reasons for using, 129–130
role of e-mail in, 125–126
use of by regulators, 129
discussion boards, 194
discussion groups, abuse of, 50
disposal, 226
disposition, of e-mail, 6
Dorn, Jeffrey W., 21
drafts, rules for retaining, 102
duplicates, rules for, 102–103

Economic Espionage Act (EEA), 21
ECPA, *see* Electronic Communication
    Privacy Act
e-discovery policy
  determining one's preparedness for,
    142–143
  enforcing policies for, 146
  importance of, 140
  IT department's role in planning for,
    145
  locating files for, 143
  preparing for, 141, 144–146
  use of technology for, 144
EEA, *see* Economic Espionage Act
electronic assets, misuse of, 232
Electronic Communication Privacy Act
    (ECPA), 31
Electronic Signatures in Global and
    National Commerce Act (E-SIGN)
  on contracts and records, 109
  significance of, 109
Electronic Storage System Require-
    ments, Section 4, 112–116
  books and records in, 113
  electronic storage system in, 113
  general requirements, 112
  indexing system requirements,
    115–116
  responsibility of taxpayer, 114–115
EmailXtender, 240
e-mail
  altering, 149
  appropriate language for, 36

benefits of secure, 174–175
and confidential information, 47
as contextual medium, 36–37,
  132–133
business risks of, 152
costs of saving, 100
deleted, 133
disposing of, 101
filters, 181
as impersonal medium, 39
as legal evidence, 28, 108, 112, 120,
  122, 133
in legal proceedings, 107, 116, 151
limitations of, 44, 173
misconceptions about, 122
parts of, 111
and password security, 150
personal use of, 46, 58
power of, 38
problems of unmanaged, 132
repudiation via, 111
retention and deletion, 70
security, 152, 154
uniqueness of, 78
user management of, 8
e-mail abuse
  by administrative assistants, 17
  adult content as, 4
  offenders of, 3
  primary types of, 5–6
  statistics of, 3, 12
e-mail content
  inappropriate language in, 33
  policy statement for, 35
  subject matter to avoid in, 34–35
  ways of controlling, 37
e-mail management
  analysis of, 10
  holistic approach to, 4
  legal strategy for, 133–134
  self-assessment of, 9–10, 120–121
e-mail mismanagement
  analysis of, 14
  self-assessment, 13
e-mail policy
  ambiguous language in, 58
  clarity in, 59
  important points for, 32
  inconsistent enforcement of, 57

ineffectiveness of written, 12–13
e-mail rules
  applied to automation, 92
  list of, 6–8
  pertaining to content, 27
  for remote workers, 52
e-mail transactions, unauthorized, 22
employees, instilling policy ownership
  in, 212
employee conduct, 19
encryption technology
  description of, 176
  need for, 174
Enron, Corp, investigation of, 136
ENTERPRISEsuite, 239
ePolicy Institute, The, 237
e-risk management
  areas of focus for, 16–17
  customer service policy as, 17
  elements of, 163
  employee education in, 207,
    215–216
  key players in, 15–16
  manager's support for, 209
  methodology of, 14
  self-assessment for, 18–19, 120–121
  strategic planning for, 14–15
E-SIGN, see Electronic Signatures in
    Global and National Commerce
    Act
evidence
  destruction of, 129
  important points regarding, 137–138
  non-litigation requirements for, 128
  paper and electronic, 128
  penalties for destroying, 135–136
  possible e-mail related, 126–127
  preserving, 136
  steps for employee handling of,
    139–141

FDA, see Food and Drug Administra-
    tion
Federal Rules of Civil Procedure
    (F.R.Civ.P.), 127, 145
filtering software, controlling content
    with, 35, 181
firewall, 160
flame, definition of, 40

Flynn, Nancy, 237
Food and Drug Administration (FDA)
    on retaining e-records, 129
F.R.Civ.P, *see* Federal Rules of Civil
    Procedure

Gartner Group
    On IM, 188
    on spam, 179
grammar, 42

hostile work environment, 18

inbound messages, security of, 167
instant messaging (IM)
    appeal of, 187
    business concerns of, 188
    important points to consider about,
        190–191
    managing, 188–189
    policies on, 189–190
    retention of, 191
    and security, 190
    technical features of, 187–188
integrity, of e-mail, 163
Internal Revenue Service (IRS)
    Electronic Storage System Require-
        ment, 112–116
    on e-records, 88
International Data Corp (IDC)
    on bandwidth problems, 181
    on business e-mail volume, 64
    on global e-mail use, 162
    on spam, 179
IDC, *see* International Data Corp
Iron Mountain, 239
IRS, *see* Internal Revenue Service

Kahn Consulting, Inc., 236, 238
Kahn, Randolph A., 236, 238
key-based security, 176–177
Klez virus, 151

language, appropriate, 36
laptop theft
    Persian Gulf War example of, 53
    statistics on, 52
large institutions
    e-mail policies of, 30–31
    workplace policies of, 27

legal
    assessment of exposure, 123–125
    risks, 151
    strategy, 133–134
Legato Systems, Inc., 240
LISTSERV
    dangers of, 49–50
    definition of, 49
    importance of rules for, 51
    statistics on popularity of, 51
Lockheed Martin, spam problem at,
    181

management, goals of e-mail, 97
management software
    benefits of, 92
    functions of, 91–92
metadata, 8, 128
MIMEsweeper, 239
mobile e-mail, types of, 193
monitoring software, 35

Napster, Inc., 199
NASD, *see* National Association of
    Securities Dealers
National Association of Securities
    Dealers (NASD)
    on business e-mail retention, 79, 129
    on use of instant messaging, 191
netiquette
    guidelines for employees, 39–44
    guidelines for managers, 45–48
    purpose of, 38
networking, 198
network security, 160
newsgroups, 195
nonrepudiation, 175

online discussion groups, abuse of, 50
online shopping, as e-risk, 16
outbound e-mail, handling security risk
    of, 172
outsourcing
    rules of, 94–96
    types of services, 96

"packet sniffers," 165
paper approach to retention, 85–87,
    225–226

passwords, 158, 230
maintenance of, 158
peer-to-peer (P2P) networking, 198,
199
risks of, 200–201
technology for, 199–200
personal contact, over e-mail, 48
personal use, of e-mail, 46, 58, 214,
230
physical security
around one's organization, 159
goal of, 157
policy
ambiguous language in, 58
clarity in, 59
important points for a, 32
inconsistent enforcement of, 57
ineffectiveness of written, 12–13
samples of, 229–235
privacy, on e-mail, 230
privacy policies
in France, 30
U.S. law regarding, 30
privacy statement, example of a, 31–32
prohibited content, in e-mails, 231
proprietary information, theft of, 20
public forums
in-house, 196–197
possible rules for, 196
Public Key Infrastructure (PKI), 176

receipts, use of, 43
record ownership statement, example
of, 23
record
definition of retention of, 71
as legal evidence, 120
lifespan of, 71–72
management, 81
retention of, 77, 88
record series
definition of, 76
lifespan of, 77
"records hold" mechanism, 136, 138,
145
remote workers, e-mail rules for, 52,
53–54
repudiation
of a business agreement, 171

protecting one's organization from,
172
respondeat superior, see vicarious liability retention
approaches to, 83–86
autoclassification for, 89
cons of digital, 84–85
cons of paper approach, 86–87
costs of, 100
details of digital, 84
of e-mail, 6, 70
employee compliance of, 98–99,
103, 104
European law on, 88
importance of formal rules for, 99
IRS requirements for, 88
legal aspects of paper, 87
paper approach to, 85–86
principles of, 78
program, 72–73
pros of digital, 83–84
pros of paper approach, 86
of records, 71, 77, 81
by regulatory bodies, 80
timespan for, 77
retention schedule
contents of, 76–77
definition of, 76
employee compliance of, 98–99,
103, 222–228
risk management
areas of focus for, 16–17
customer service policy as, 17
elements of, 163, 170–171
key players in, 15–16
methodology of, 14
self-assessment for, 18–19, 120–121
strategic planning for, 14–15

salutations, 41
sample policies, 229–235
sample rules, 225–227
Securities and Exchange Commission
(SEC)
on business e-mail retention, 79, 94,
129
e-mail requirements for media and
process, 79–80
SEC, see Securities and Exchange Commission

secure e-mail gateways, 177
security
  breech of information, 155
  cipher and, 176
  of content, 162–163
  continual process of, 153
  decryption and, 176
  encryption and, 176
  factors in developing policies for,
    178
  key-based, 176–177
  laws regarding, 155
  of network, 160
  physical, 157
  physical and network considerations
    for, 160–161
  policies for, 156
  Public Key Infrastructure and, 176
  risks assessment, 154
  secrets of, 152
  use of passwords for, 158
  Web-based, 177
self-destructing e-mail, see self-erasing
  e-mail
self-erasing e-mail, use of, 137
Service Level Agreement (SLA), issues
  addressed in, 95
sexual harassment
  employer responsibility in, 55–56
  poor handling of, 56
short messaging service (SMS), 192
  business appeal of, 193
  difficulty of retention, 193–194
signatures, 41–42
SMS, see short messaging service
spam
  characteristics of, 182
  direct marketing use of, 180
  eliminating, 183
  Gartner Group on, 179
  handling, 40–41
  organizational handling of, 181
  statistics on, 179
  workplace liabilities caused by,
    180–181
SSPs, see Storage Service Providers

standards, for e-mail usage, 234–235
Statement Against Interest, 28
storage, issues with employee, 97
Storage Service Providers (SSPs)
  definition of, 93
system administrators, 158

technology department, questions for,
  124
technology experts, court use of, 131
time management, electronic, 8
training, 208–211, 213–215
training manual, 209–210
transactions, unauthorized, 22
transmission, of e-mail, 7
Trojan horses, 165

Uniform Electronic Commerce Act
  (UETA)
  on retention of electronic records,
    110
  significance of, 109
UETA, see Uniform Electronic Commerce Act
unsolicited messages, handling, 35
U.S. Department of Justice, on trade secret theft, 21
U.S. Supreme Court
  on corporate defense against hostile
    work environment, 18
  rulings on corporate liability, 56

vicarious liability,
  definition of, 55
viruses
  definition of, 164
  detecting, 166–167
  educating employees about, 165–166
  hoax, 165
  self-propagating, 164
  targets of, 164

Web-based
  e-mail, 202–203
  message boards, 195
Web server, 199
worm, 165

About the Authors

Nancy Flynn is founder and executive director of The ePolicy Institute™, dedicated to helping employers reduce e-risks, while enhancing employees' e-mail writing skills. Through the ePolicy Institute Speakers' Bureau, Flynn speaks and conducts online and on-site training worldwide. Recognized for her e-policy and e-mail expertise, Flynn has been featured in the *Wall Street Journal, US News & World Report,* USAtoday.com, *Training,* and National Public Radio, among thousands of media outlets worldwide. Published in four languages, Flynn is the author of *The ePolicy Handbook* (AMACOM), *Writing Effective E-Mail,* and other books. To book Nancy Flynn as a speaker or consultant, visit The ePolicy Institute at www.ePolicyInstitute.com, or contact Flynn directly via phone, fax, or snail mail.

Randolph Kahn is an attorney and internationally recognized authority on the legal, risk management, retention, and policy issues of business information and records management. As founder and principal of Kahn Consulting, Inc., www.Kahn ConsultingInc.com, Kahn leads a team of consultants who advise corporations and governmental agencies on a wide range of issues related to information and electronic records management. He has played an important role in the development of industry standards related to electronic records, e-business risk management, information security, and information management. Each year, Kahn conducts dozens of seminars and training programs for corporate and government institutions. He is an instructor at George Washington University and a columnist for an information technology magazine. Kahn has authored numerous articles for legal, industry, and mainstream publications and is interviewed by a wide variety of media outlets regularly.

To book a speaker, consultant, or media interview, contact:

Nancy Flynn
The ePolicy Institute.
nancy@epolicyinstitute.com
www.epolicyinstitute.com
614-451-3200

Randolph Kahn, Esq.
Kahn Consulting, Inc.
RKahn@KahnConsultingInc.com
847-266-0722
www.KahnConsultingInc.com

Printed in the United States
62481LVS00003B/1-108